bev bos

Chants,
Fingerplays
& Stories

*Have fun Chord!
Michael
Leeman*

Compiled and Illustrated by
Michael Leeman

Turn the Page Press, Inc.
ROSEVILLE CA

Published by
Turn the Page Press, Inc.
900 Church Street
Roseville CA 95678
(800)-959-5549
www.turnthepage.com

ISBN 0-931793-05-X

Printed by
Paul Baker Printing
220 Riverside Ave
Roseville CA 95678
(916) 783-8317
www.pbaker.com

Cover design Michael Leeman

Acknowledgments -

We would like to acknowledge with gratitude the many teachers who over the years have generously shared
their stories and talents with us. Their willingness to collaborate with colleagues is symbolic of the teaching
profession and of storytellers, too. To list the many fine storytellers we have been influenced by would be a
daunting task but would certainly include Anne Pellowski, Margaret Read McDonald, Bill Gordh, and Pete
Seeger.

Dirty Bill from Vinegar Hill reprinted with permission of the author, Aubrey Davis. *The Sleeping Bag Chant*
reprinted with permission of the author, Linnea Goode.

Our special thanks to Roseville Community Preschool teachers, Sally Hupp, Kelly Anderson and Cheryl
Roesser, for their assistance.

_____

Other books from Turn the Page Press, Inc.

Don't Move the Muffin Tins - a hands-off guide to art for young children - Bev Bos

Together We're Better - establishing a coactive learning environment - Bev Bos

Tumbling Over the Edge - a rant for children's play - Bev Bos & Jenny Chapman

Morningtown Ride (Children's Book) - Illustrated by Michael Leeman

Chants & Fingerplays

glumly at the storyteller and their movements are slow and deliberate. How very different from when the kids -- right from the start -- are invited into the creative process and you look up and see twenty-five individual reactions to the same words.

After having worked with children for four decades, Bev has become very adept at paying attention to any little utterance that a child may say and immediately turning it into a simple song or chant. A good example of this involves the chant Chocolate Candy and Jelly Beans. It came about one day at preschool when a child reached into his pants pocket and realized that whatever it was that he felt in his hand, it had obviously gone through the washing machine. Bev took that moment (which otherwise might have been embarrassing for the child) and turned it into a chant that the other children and adults could relate to -- in a sensitive and marvelous way. Everyone has made a mistake at one time or another, but to turn it around to where it becomes a celebration of being human can happen when you practice making chants and fingerplays and stories part of your life.

Over the years, as we have worked with children, we have enjoyed learning and sharing many chants and stories. This book is our collection of "winners." Please don't get too caught up in the memorizing and such that your own creativity suffers. We realize some of you who may not have grown up hearing chants, fingerplays and stories, or may have forgotten them over the years, so we have added our comments and suggestions to help you get started. Please take advantage of the experience we have to offer but as soon as you become comfortable and practiced at the craft, we hope you will strike out on your own by creating or adapting these chants, fingerplays and stories -- and discovering some of your own, too. Nothing would please us more than to hear, "We've been using your book and the children have changed every one of them!" You will probably notice that some of the chants and stories in this book are just as you heard them years before and some may be unfamiliar or only slightly unrecognizable as we have adapted them. This kind of "license" plays a vital role in keeping the oral tradition alive and well. When you can credit the author of the story. If it is unknown, just preface it with "this is one I heard when I was your age."

So, use these stories and chants with kids and personalize them, add to them, or subtract. It is our hope that you and the children in your care will become stewards in the preservation of the increasingly endangered art of fingerplays, chants and stories.

Preface for the Reader

As a preschool teacher, there's nothing like having a new chant or fingerplay when Monday morning rolls around. We know all too well that it's what can keep the fires burning, the juices flowing and the spirit alive for the children and for the teacher, too. The children can often tell by the look on our faces when we have something new to share with them. There is an air of anticipation on everyone's part to "get on with it." It's the same for parents, too. There isn't a child alive that hasn't in some way beseeched the adults in their life with, "tell me a story."

We've been doing this long enough to know, immediately upon hearing a new chant, if it's a winner or not. At first there's great anticipation followed by a few hours of practice, maybe a little fine tuning of the words or actions, before we throw it out to the kids. Our first bit of advice is don't wait until you have a new chant or story down pat. Use the first few times of actually doing it as your rehearsal. Most children really don't care how well you do it, their focus is on "what's in it for me" not on your performance. Remember this when you are considering a new story or chant; is its focus on the participation of the audience or on the teller's performance?

Our next suggestion is to embrace creative power of serendipity. There is great value in the spontaneity of witnessing something coming to life before your eyes. So be courageous. To accomplish that you will have to be open to new ideas and suggestions from the children. Besides the great pleasure for all involved when everyone participates, the children benefit by being allowed to make the chants and stories their own. The more a child has ownership over moments like shared story, the more likely they are to continue participating in the oral tradition and to carry with them these playful memories. Let these moments serve as the overture to the symphony that is to be the child's literate life.

Accept that all of your attempts will not necessarily meet with success. We, too, have experienced our share of rejection after spending all weekend prepping only to have the next great thing fall totally flat with the kids. Most everyone has. But, then next week the same chant is a huge hit. In the world of working with children we have to remain incredibly flexible. When introducing a new chant or story be judicious with your level of direction. Do not use as a measure of success whether all the children are doing it right. This can have a stifling affect on the children's creativity. We have witnessed children in classrooms or in concert settings where the children seem so intent on not making a mistake that they become oblivious to the story itself. The children stare imaginations." In this one-on-one storytelling we experience the joy of sharing a story *with someone* rather than telling a story *to* someone.

Whether true or pure fantasy, stories offered us a chance to imagine situations and to scoff at, to hiss or cheer for, or be amazed and mesmerized by these histories or legends and their protagonists. Most importantly of all for children, stories provided the chance to form pictures on the walls of their mind. Even though we didn't know it at the time, the more we played and heard and experienced fingerplays, chants and stories via the oral tradition, the more eager, stimulated and prepared we were when the time was right for the reading and writing chapter of our literate lives to burst forth.

Our purpose for writing this book is our belief that fingerplays, chants and the telling of stories during the early years of a child's home-life are in danger of becoming a lost art. Their value having been greatly diminished, their role becoming almost nonexistent in childhoods that are dominated by visually compelling devices and electronic gizmos. More and more, families are relying on machines when it comes to keeping company with children. The human voice, the parent's voice, many times is no longer the one a child comes to count on for consoling and cajoling, for reviving and inspiring, for introducing the child to family history, artifacts, and traditions. These things are best conveyed to the child through sound -- words spoken and sung.

There needs to be a rebirth or revitalization of this part of the oral tradition. Tragically, its importance during the childhood years far too many people now label as old-fashion and out-of-date. The children of today are more likely to find themselves hurried through their childhood prematurely inundated in pages and letters. As author Barry Sanders writes in his book *A is for Ox - The Collapse of Literacy and the Rise of Violence in an Electronic Age*, "A child who has not grown up in the bosom of orality . . . approaches reading and writing with caution or suspicion -- as a brand new and alien processes -- rather than coming to them with enthusiasm . . . Children need to hear language in order to learn language." This all begins with the first sighs and babbles between mother and child.

Part of the richness inherent in fingerplay, chants and stories is that for each person who listens, there is a personal reaction -- one all their own. Stories can speak to us in several ways at once. When we come back to the same story after a time, sometimes it will tell us new things. With playful child-like energy we find these stories and games to be great fun. But, sadly, their connection to the words "play" and "fun" can often eclipse the deep, meaningful aspect of this pursuit. We should take great care not to view as frivolous their benefit to the well-being of children. We must hold firmly to both the precious and the purpose in the brief time that we get to keep company with our children.

Introduction

How many of you have experienced a moment when someone says or does something that triggers a memory of a time, now long in the past, when you did some simple little thing like a fingerplay or word game when you were young? Perhaps it conjured up a memory of you, and someone close to you, telling a story at bedtime or playing a game while on a long car trip. For some of you it may be the memory of sitting in church and your fidgeting and squirming resulted in a handkerchief mouse magically appearing from the vest pocket of your grandfather's suit. Or, maybe a visiting aunt or an uncle, whom you had never even met, had broken the ice with a playful game of peek-a-boo, or your Mother pat-a-caking her way through dressing you for school, or as a group of school aged kids, your jump rope chants clapped out a rhythm to your adolescent allegiances. And now, thinking back on such moments, you can easily provide vivid details about how old you were, the people who were with you, the smells, the sounds, the feelings of closeness and the particulars of the stories or games themselves.

". . . here is Grandpa's looking glass, and here's the baby's cradle, rock, rock."
"Down by the banks of the Hankie Pankie, where the bullfrogs jump from. . ."

How these playful little creations got their start, who could know. But, thankfully, over the years families passed them down with each generation making them their own with adaptations here and there. It seems, what ever form they took, they were part of nearly every parent's and grandparents's bag of tricks. They were also part of the repetoire of teachers, too. These seemingly unsophisticated little games and rhymes are arguably, quite sophisticated; the word's root coming from the Sophists of ancient Greece, a group of teachers characterized by their cleverness. How clever in their perfection are these little games at infusing moments between adult and child with an intimacy that hooks itself to the mind and body and remains intact the whole life long.

Fingerplays, however brief, were often the very first stories we experienced. With our hands we gave shape to the words, our fingers could come to symbolize many different things and, in their telling, those stories literally became part of our body. And, what about our toes? How many of them in the hands of countless generations of parents were transformed by the words, "this little piggy . . . ?"

Chants started us on the road to poetry with their meter and rhyme, patterns and language. Stories, from the mouths of adults to the ears of the young, the benefits of which have been well documented over the years, are in the words of storyteller Margaret Read McDonald, the "gift of shared

Table of Contents

CHANTS & FINGERPLAYS

To Carrie, Meghan and Jillian for their patient posing and for so graciously enduring the burden of living with an artist.

-- M. L.

For my mother -- Helen.

-- B. B.

The Baby Chant -

Now's the time to go to sleep,

Put the baby in the bed,

Cover the baby in the bed,

And kiss the baby "Goodnight." (Kiss!)

birch

To follow the last line with, "Oh, no, the baby's out of bed! We must have forgotten something!" -- turns this sweet chant into a cumulative tale about a baby that keeps getting out of bed as everyone tries to figure out why. This chant draws out many varied responses from the children. Some might add, "give the baby it's bottle" or "a drink of water" or "find the pacifier" or "blanket" and "change the baby's diaper" "tell the baby a story." We love that their responses also offer the children personal glimpses of how other families cope with wide awake babies.

Michael: *When Bev taught me this chant, I used it that day with the school-age kids I work with. Their responses were a bit of a surprise until I reminded myself that, at this age, their focus is on problem-solving. Whereas the younger kids were more concerned about taking care of the baby's needs, the answers from the older ones dealt mainly with keeping that baby in bed! Here are some of the answers they gave:*
>   *"Lock the cradle!" and*
>   *"Chain the baby down!"*

One girl insinuated that I was the reason the baby kept getting out of bed! She said, "I've been watching you. When you kiss the baby, you take all the covers off" (meaning I was opening my hand all the way when I kissed my finger). She advised, "Maybe if you just take a little bit of the covers off, (just one finger rather than opening my hand all the way) kiss the baby and sneak out of the room and then the baby won't wake up!"

Once, I told the kids that "at my house I'm usually the first one to fall asleep at night. So, sometimes one of my grown children will show me to bed! So, now what would do you do when you have a dad who gets out of bed!?!" They yelled, "Make him a sandwich" "get him a snack" and you can always count on roars of laughter as invariably the kids will suggest "give the daddy a bottle" or "give the daddy a pacifier!"

(continued on next page)

To start the chant, hold one open hand in front of you with palm up (this is the bed),
close the other hand except for the index finger, pointing up (this is the baby).

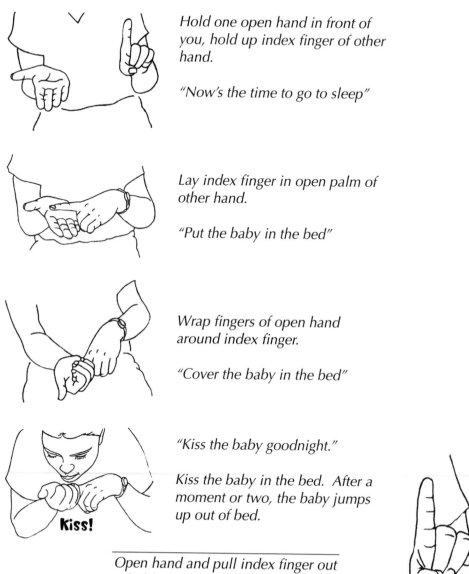

Hold one open hand in front of
you, hold up index finger of other
hand.

"Now's the time to go to sleep"

Lay index finger in open palm of
other hand.

"Put the baby in the bed"

Wrap fingers of open hand
around index finger.

"Cover the baby in the bed"

"Kiss the baby goodnight."

Kiss the baby in the bed. After a
moment or two, the baby jumps
up out of bed.

Kiss!

Open hand and pull index finger out
-- holding upright.

*"Uh oh, the baby's out of bed! We
must have forgotten something!"*

Bananas, Coconuts & Grapes? -

I like bananas, coconuts and grapes,
I like bananas, coconuts and grapes,
I like bananas, coconuts and grapes,
That's why they call me Tarzan of the apes.

Use your hands to create the shapes of the fruits bananas, coconuts and grapes and for the last line we pound on our chests and say, "That's why they call me Tarzan of the Apes!" What other fruits or vegetables can we do?

The Swing by Robert Louis Stevenson

How do you like to go up in swing,
Up in the air so blue?
"Oh, I do think it the pleasantest thing
Ever a child can do!"

"Up in the air and over the wall,
Till I can see so wide,
Rivers and trees and cattle and all
Over the countyside.

"Till I look down on the garden green
Down on the roof so brown,
Up in the air I go flying again,
Up in the air and down!"

horse

chestnut

Benji -

aspen

This chant is fun to do with all ages -- especially older children and adults. It also works well when done as a round. When each group knows their part well, they can move around the room as they do the round. This great suggestion comes to us from our friend, Tom Hunter.

Benji met the Bear, the Bear met Benji,

The Bear was bulgy, the bulge was Benji.

Benji . . . . . . .met the Bear,

The Bear . . . . . . met Benji,

The Bear . . . . . . was bulgy,

The bulge . . . . . was Benji.

Big Green Monster -

There's a big, green monster under my bed,

With a floppy face sticking out of his head,

With one foot up and the other foot down,

He swings his hips around and around,

His face he gets all scrunched up, too,

And that ugly beast looks a lot like you!

This chant is an echo, or answer-back, chant. As you say each line, the children repeat it as well as doing what he big, green monster does.

. . . and that ugly beast . . .

. . . looks alot like you!

A funny thing happened to my sister Letty,
Instead of hair, she grew spaghetti,
And now when she gets hungry at night,
She combs some down and takes a bite.

holly

The Bunny Chant -

sassafras

Here's a little bunny,

Sitting in the sun,

Along comes a little dog,

Watch that bunny run!

Chocolate Candy & Jelly Beans -

Chocolate candy and jelly beans,

Put 'em in my pockets,

Put 'em in my jeans,

Mama washed the clothes,

And then my Mama said, (Aauugghh!)

"Chocolate candy and jelly beans,

All over my washing machine!"

Bev: *We pat our hands on our thighs to give a beat to the chant. The children usually act out the "put 'em in my pockets - put 'em in my jeans" and for the "Aauugghh! they wave their hands over their heads. There are answers that always find their way into this chant when we ask "What have you left in your pockets?" -- Tissues, gum, money, candy . . . I love that this chant is so real. It's something all children have experienced*

Couldn't Sleep Last Night -

An answer back chant that grows by adding a new line with each succeeding verse. Songs about nighttime are especially "real" to young children -- most of whom have spent many hours awake in a dark bedroom listening to the sounds of the night.

One, two, three, four,   [One, two, three, four]

One, two, three, four,   [One, two, three, four]

Couldn't sleep last night,   [couldn't sleep last night]

With the thunder and the lightning, [with the thunder and the lightning]

And the dog on the bed,   [and the dog on the bed]

And the chicken in the kitchen, [and the chicken in the kitchen]

At the Barn Bell Farm.   [at the Barn Bell Farm]

(Over the years the children added the following lines. Add them in one by one, repeating the rest of the chant as you go).

Couldn't sleep last night, with my daddy snoring . . . (with the thunder and . . .)

Couldn't sleep last night, with the baby crying . . . (with my daddy snoring . . .)

Couldn't sleep last night, with the cows mooing . . . (with the baby crying . . .)

Couldn't sleep last night, with the horns honking . . . (with the cows mooing . . .)

One, two, three, four . . . (repeat three times)   Sssshhhhhhh.

> I saw Johnny floatin' down the Delaware,
>
> Hole in his underwear, couldn't buy another pair,
>
> Three weeks later bitten by a polar bear,
>
> The poor old Polar bear died.

The Damper Chant -

You push the damper in,

And you pull the damper out,

And the smoke goes up the chimney,

Just the same, just the same,

And the smoke goes up the chimney,

Just the same.

With this chant we drop off the words but continue to act them out. First we leave off "in" then the next time through we drop "in" and "out" and then finally, all three "in, out and smoke" but continue to do the hand motions.

Diddle Diddle Dum -

This is a chant we do while watching the children demonstrate whatever they choose to do, like spin, jump, crawl, hop, wiggle . . . We ask, "What are you going to do now? And while they do it, we chant, "Diddle diddle dum, diddle diddle dum, hoopla wee, hoopla wee, little children having more fun than me!" Here are some hand motions we have added over the years.

Diddle diddle dum,

Diddle diddle dum,

Hoopla wee, hoopla wee,

Little children having more

fun than me.

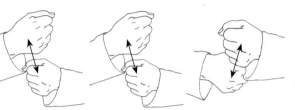

Diddle ....diddle................dum

Hoopla wee.............hoopla wee

Dirty Bill from Vinegar Hill -

[Chorus]
Scrub scrub -- Splash splash splash
Scrub scrub -- Splash splash splash
　I'm Dirty Bill from Vinegar Hill.
　I never had a bath and I never will!
　I'm Dirty Bill from Vinegar Hill.
　I never had a bath and I never will!

Catch him!
Snatch him!
Put him in the tub.
Pour in the water.
Rub a dub dub. [Chorus]

Put him in the bath tub!
Put him in the sink!
Wash away the dirt!
And the stink, stink, stink. [Chorus]

Bubbles in his hair
Soapsuds on his hide.
From front to back
And side to side. [Chorus]

Soap him up.
Scrub him down.
Wash him.
Rinse him
Round and round. [Chorus]

Scrub scrub -- Splash splash splash
Scrub scrub -- Splash splash splash.
Scrub scrub -- Splash splash splash

Blub, blub blub -- Blub blub blub
Blub

Bev: A great chant from Aubrey Davis, that our kids have had a lot of fun with. The first time we did this chant at preschool, we got to the end and a boy immediately jumped up and yelled, "DO MY DAD!" I said, "You mean, Russ?" He said, "Yeah, and he lives in Sacramento!"

　He's Dirty Russ from Sacramento.
　He never had a bath and he never will.

You can imagine what happened next. All the children insisted that we put all their relatives in the chant, too. Moms, brothers, sisters, grandparents . . . etc. A great example of how children become engaged by making the chant their own.

As you can probably tell, this chant is perfect for acting out the words, too. Have fun!

Don't Touch the Baby -

ash

Hold one hand up in front of you with fingers spread apart. The thumb and fingers of the hand form the members of the family with the pinky finger being the baby. Start the chant by introducing the members of the family.

This is the Mother,	*Point to thumb.*
This is the Father,	*Point to index finger.*
And this is the Brother tall,	*Point to middle finger.*
This is the Sister,	*Point to ring finger.*
And this is the Baby.	*Point to little finger.*
The mother says, "Don't touch the baby!"	*Point to thumb - (then wag finger)*
The father says, "Don't touch the baby!"	*Point to index finger . . .*
The brother says, "Don't touch the baby!"	*Point to middle finger . . .*
The sister says, "Don't touch the baby!"	*Point to ring finger . . .*
"Which one is the baby?"	*(When person reaches for little finger to point to it, jerk the hand away and saying: "DON'T TOUCH THE BABY!"*
"DON'T TOUCH THE BABY!"	

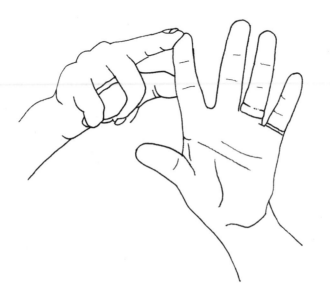

Five Little Monkeys -

Five little monkeys sittin' in a tree,

Teasing Mr. Alligator, saying,

"You can't catch me!"

(Chomp)

Four little monkeys . . .

Three little monkeys . . .

Two little monkeys . . .

One little monkey sittin' in a tree,

Teasing Mr. Alligator, saying,

"You can't catch me!"

(Chomp)

No little monkeys . . .

. . . sitting in a tree.

Occasionally, it is brought up that some chants or stories are too scary for young children. According to famed psychoanalyst Maria von Franz, these kind of stories serve to bring out into the open the child's worst fears. It gives them the chance to confront scary things in the presence of their parents or teachers. Further, it lets them know that they are not the only ones to harbor such fears and worries.

When you do chants, fingerplay and stories that have scary subject matter of events, and allow the children to voice their reactions or ask questions, you are providing a tremendous service to the young people in your care.

Chomp!

hickory

Five Little Peas -

catalpa

> Five little peas,
>
> In a pea pod pressed,
>
> One grew, two grew,
>
> And so did all the rest,
>
> They grew and they grew,
>
> And they did not stop,
>
> They grew so big,
>
> That the pea pod popped!   (continued on next page)

Michael: *"They grew so big that the pea pod popped!" The perfect finish to a really fun chant. The kids love the clapping and especially the anticipation of timing their final clap to coincide with the end of the chant. The meter of this little poem is just perfect -- you can almost feel it in your bones as it bounces along.*

A common suggestion children offer after hearing the chant is that if FIVE little peas was that much fun, TEN would be much, much better! And ONE HUNDRED -- far better still. It's easy -- we do the chant the same way except when we get to "one grew, two grew, and so did all the rest" we just as quickly as we can flash our fingers five or ten at a time as we pretend to count to whatever number was suggested. And, occasionally, the children clap to number of peas, instead of the number of pods. Which is just a reminder to us adults that the clapping is the part the kids really love.

> I eat my peas with honey,
>
> I've done it all my life,
>
> It makes the peas taste funny,
>
> But, it keeps them on my knife.
>
> - Unknown

Five little peas,   *In a pea pod pressed,*   *One grew,*   *Two grew,*

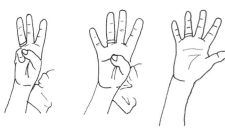 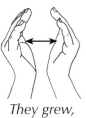 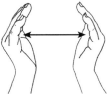

And so ....did all ....the rest,   *They grew,*   *and they grew,*

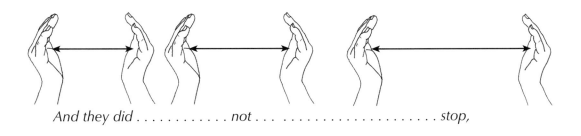

And they did . . . . not . . . . stop,

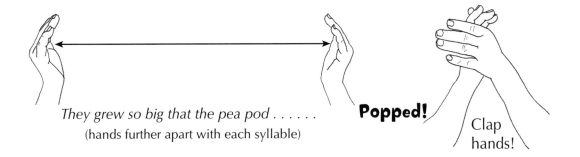

They grew so big that the pea pod . . . . . .
(hands further apart with each syllable)

Popped!

Clap
hands!

Gimme Five -

Gimme five,

Other side,

Cut the pickle,

Get a tickle.

willow

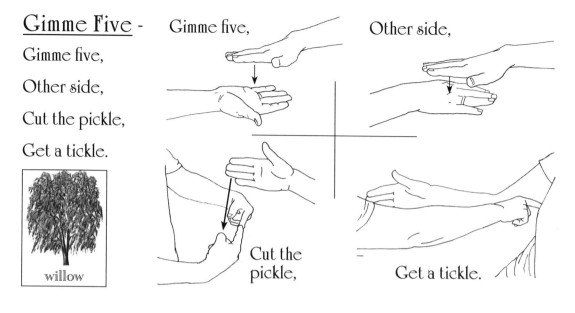

Gimme five,

Other side,

Cut the
pickle,

Get a tickle.

(four more) Give a Tickle Chants -

'Round and 'round the cornfield,

Looking for a hare,

Where can we find one?

Right up there!

    Can you feel this little spider,

    Dancing in your hand?

    Now, he goes to the top of the hill,

    And he runs back down again.

Round about, round about,

Ran the wee mouse,

Up a bit, up a bit,

Into his wee house.

    Round and round the orchard,

    Buzzed a little bee,

    To tend to springtime's flowers,

    She flits from tree to tree.

Here are some great "one-on-one" games to play with young children. In each one, there is the opportunity to run up the child's arm with your hand for a quick little tickle under the arm or chin. Most children will scrunch up and pull their hand away out of reflex and as soon as the laughter dies down, they say, "do it again!" So, to keep from having to do the same one over and over, here are four more to add to your collection. To old favorites and two new ones.

<u>Grassy, Grass, Grass</u> - (Cloudy, Cloud, Cloud)

Bev: *I have always been surprised at how successful this simple little chant has been with the children. Once you get it started the children will start throwing words and ideas into the middle of the sweet chant and it just keeps rolling along. I always start the chant with:* ⟶

Cloudy ... cloud cloud,

Rainy ... rainy rain,

Muddy ... muddy mud,

Windy ... windy wind,

It is usually about this point of the chant that the kids take over. We almost always pat our hands on our laps as we do this chant, too. We have written the chant in way that might help you understand the fun cadence we use. We pause after the first word and then say the last two together in quick succession as you pat along to that rhythm.

Here are lyrics to a similar song/chant attributed to Woody Guthrie:

Grass grass grass
Tree tree tree
Leafy leafy leaf
One two three

Doggie doggie dog
Runny run run
Quickie quick quick
Homey home home

Birdy birdy bird
Fly fly fly
Nest nest nest
High high high

Beddy bed bed
Sheety sheet sheet
Sleep sleep sleep
Dreamy dreamy dream

Cloudy cloudy cloud
Wind wind wind
Rain rain rain
Mud mud mud

Dancie dance dance
Singy sing sing
Grow grow grow
Biggy big big

wild
cherry

Gobble Gobble Turkey -

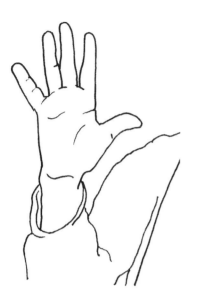

box elder

Gobble, gobble. says Mr. Turkey,

It's almost Thanksgiving Day,

How will you treat me?

Will you eat me?

Then I have to run away.

Michael: *Ever notice how many finger-plays embody the essence of the real world of young children -- that things are constantly going away and coming back? They go to sleep and wake in new day, mom leaves the room and now she's back, or they left me at school, I hope they come back for me. Just like that ole Gobble Turkey -- it was just here and now it's gone! Where did it go? Many of these chants also deal with the cycle of life and occasionally, children will take the opportunity to bring up things that concern them.*

Grandma's Glasses -

Here are Grandma's glasses, here is Grandma's hat,

And here's the way she folds her hands, just like that.

Here are Grandpa's glasses, here's his big, tall hat,

And here's the way he folds his arms, just like that.

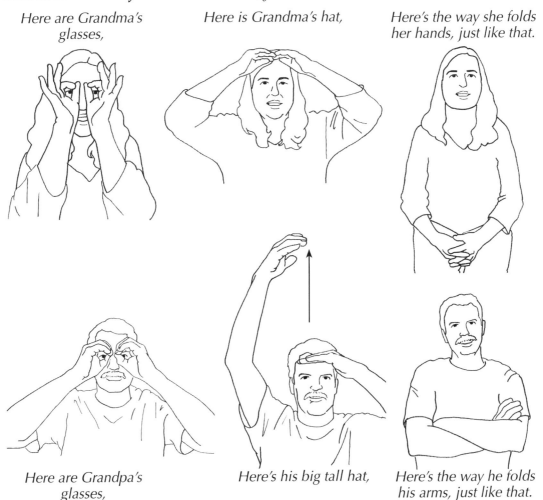

Here are Grandma's glasses,

Here is Grandma's hat,

Here's the way she folds her hands, just like that.

Here are Grandpa's glasses,

Here's his big tall hat,

Here's the way he folds his arms, just like that.

A question I might pose to the children: "What kind of hat would you wear? Their answers might be: "my mom's hat," "the hat I wear to the snow," "a wild and crazy hat," " sunglasses," We end each with "and here's the way we fold our arms . . ."

Grandma's Knives & Forks -

Bev: *I've known this chant since I was 3 or 4 years old. I encourage you to think back to your own childhoods when looking for chants and fingerplays. There is something powerful in inviting children into your life by allowing them a glimpse of your childhood, too.*

Here are Grandma's knives and forks,

And here is Grandpa's table,

Here is Brother's looking glass,

And here's the Baby's cradle.

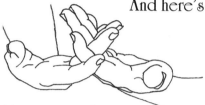

Here are grandma's
knives and forks,

And, here is
grandpa's table,

Here is brother's
looking glass,

And, here's the baby's
cradle. Rock, rock.

With this chant we change the players with each telling -- such as, "here are sister's knives and forks and here is Uncle's table . . ." or you can substitute the names of the children participating with you. A wonderful chant to play around with. In fact, we rarely do this one the same way twice -- except that we always end with, "and here's the baby's cradle."

Here's a Bunny With Ears So Funny -

cypress

Here's a bunny with ears so funny,

And here's a hole in the ground,

When a noise she hears, she picks up her ears,

And, she jumps the a hole in the ground.

This chant can be play by oneself or by two people (each taking either the role of the bunny or the hole). We have made the chant more playful by having the hole move around when it comes time for the bunny to "jump in." Also, children can use their whole body for the bunny (arms stretched up above head for "ears" and their partner making a big "hole" by using their arms. It quickly becomes a game of chase.

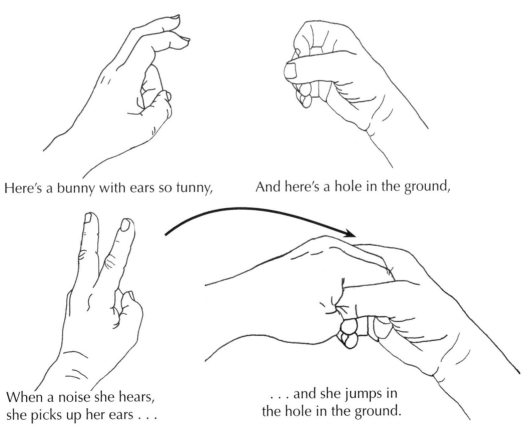

Here's a bunny with ears so funny,

And here's a hole in the ground,

When a noise she hears, she picks up her ears . . .

. . . and she jumps in the hole in the ground.

Here's The Key to Rome -

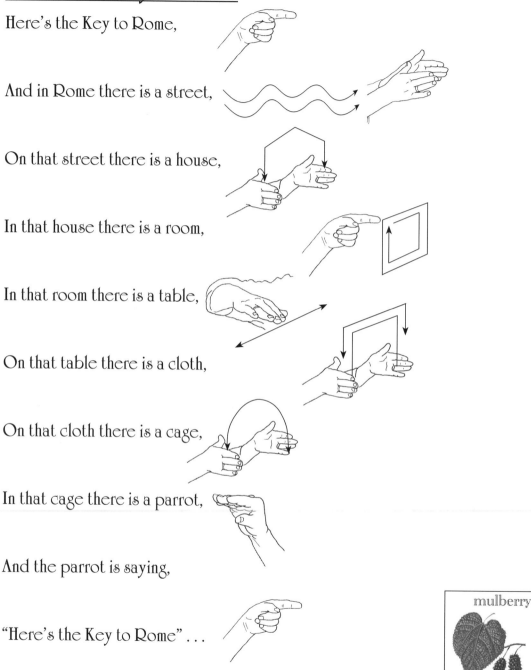

Here's the Key to Rome,

And in Rome there is a street,

On that street there is a house,

In that house there is a room,

In that room there is a table,

On that table there is a cloth,

On that cloth there is a cage,

In that cage there is a parrot,

And the parrot is saying,

"Here's the Key to Rome" . . .

mulberry

I Am Slowly Going Crazy -

I am slowly going crazy,

One, two, three, four, five, six -- switch!

Crazy going slowly am I,

Six, five, four, three, two, one -- switch!

bald cypress

Forwards and backwards this chant is a lot of fun. The younger the child, the more likely they are to switch using the same hand just moving it from cheek to cheek. Some of the children we have done this with insist on doing it faster and faster and sometimes even trying it in super slow-motion.

I am slowly going crazy,
1,2,3,4,5,6

SWITCH!

Crazy going slowly am I,
6,5,4,3,2,1 - Switch!

I Had a Little Pig -

I had a little pig,

And I fed him from a trough,

He got so big,

That his tail popped off,

So, I got me a hammer,

And I got me a nail,

And I made that piggy,

A wooden tail.

maple

(continued on next page)

This wonderful chant came to us from our friend and musician/singer Hugh Hanley. It provides a great opportunity for children to change the chant around and to dream up their own hand motions   You can do this chant using other animals, too. The kids can decide what animal, whether it is big or little, what "pops" off, which will then lead to a discussion of how many nails it will take to get "that" back on!

Michael: *About the third time we did this as a class, one of the children asked, "Can we do a different animal?" I said, "Sure, what animal do you want to do?" To which he replied, "An elephant." Okay, "I had a little elephant, I fed him from a trough, he got so big, that his . . ." (I waited for his suggestion) . . . he said, "His ears popped off!" So, I got me a hammer, and I got me a nail . . . the boy interrupted to say, "You know, I think you are going to need two nails." He was absolutely right. "So, I got me two nails, and I made that elephant some wooden ears." It's not important that it doesn't rhyme.*

This is one of the most creative chants I have ever used with young children. Recently, after involving every animal we could think, I prepared to move on to a different chant, until the children realized we could involved members of their family!

I had a little pig,

And I fed him from a trough,

He got so big,

Clap!

That his tail popped off!

So, I got me a hammer,

and I got me a nail . . .

. . . and I made that piggy a wooden tail!

Johnny Opps -

Here's a chant that requires some close observation by the children to figure out the trick. Start the chant by touching to the thumb-tip and saying "Opps." Slide your finger along the thumb to the valley between thumb and your forefinger.

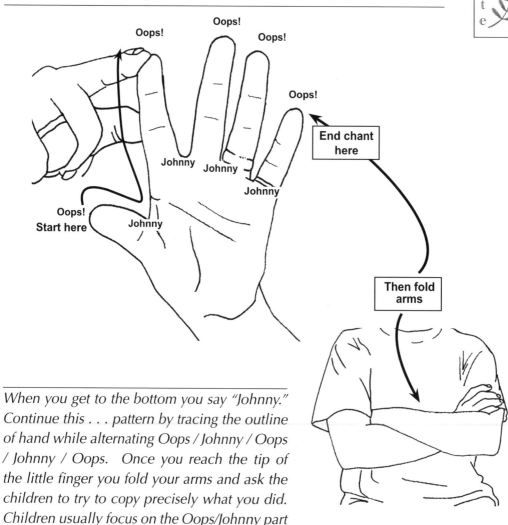

Oops!

Oops!   Oops!

Oops!

End chant here

Johnny Johnny

Johnny

Oops!
Start here   Johnny

Then fold arms

When you get to the bottom you say "Johnny." Continue this . . . pattern by tracing the outline of hand while alternating Oops / Johnny / Oops / Johnny / Oops. Once you reach the tip of the little finger you fold your arms and ask the children to try to copy precisely what you did. Children usually focus on the Oops/Johnny part of the chant -- not noticing your folded arms. As they complete their attempt to copy, you say, "You almost have it, watch close and copy everything I do." Repeat chant and fold arms. Keep doing it until someone notices the trick.

Jump in the Puddle -

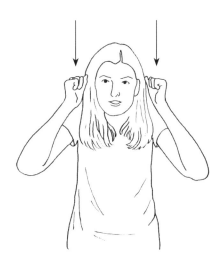

We jump, jump, jump,

In a puddle,

As the rain comes pittery pat,

We jump, jump, jump,

In a puddle,

And I pull on my coat and my hat,

Then I put up my umbrella,

And I pull on my boots with a tug, (ugh)

We jump, jump, jump,

In a puddle,

As snug as a bug in a rug.

This is a great chant for acting out the words. Not as great as doing the real thing, but certainly a satifactory substitute on those dry summer days.

Ugh!

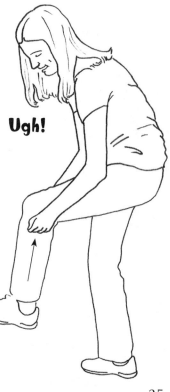

ailanthus

Jump Jim Joe -

Jump, jump, jump Jim Joe,

Shake your head,

Nod your head,

And tap your toe,

Around and around and around you go,

Find another partner and jump Jim Joe.

We have included the song Jump Jim Joe for a number of reasons. It has been tremendously popular with the children and it provides the kind of examples of how a chant or song can be changed by children and adults. The most dramatic change has been to give children the option of doing the chant by oneself or with a partner or as a group. Especially young children will run to their closest friend at he start of the chant but can quickly become upset at the prospect of having to give up that friend, and find a new one, as the chant suggests. So, we changed the last part of the chant to say, "Find another space, move to new place and . . . jump Jim Joe." Also, groups of two or three or larger can all hold hands and do the chant together or a child can choose to do it all by them self, too.

Teachers and parents, who may not be comfortable with their singing voices, often find that Jump Jim Joe can be easily chanted with no thought given to melody or musicality. This is something we encourage people to do with any song that lends it self to use with children. Children are often less concerned about your singing voice and more focused on what the chant has to offer them. In our opinion, the rhythm, movement, and the opportunity to fiddle around with the song or chant are more important than adhering to the melody. Although, sometimes your own melody can just "happen" while chanting the words to a song. The most important thing to remember is that for young children the experience is about "participation" and rarely about "performance." Our thanks to Hugh Hanley for this fine chant, too.

white pine

Keep Off the Grass -

This finger-play challenges the children to "see" or imagine as you diagram a part of any real or make-believe town. Describe the town by pointing to a place on your open palm and telling the children what you are pointing at. For example, "Here's the school and here's the grocery store and here's where I live and here's the bank . . ." etc. There is no need to be precise with each telling. The only part of the story you must include involves a park, a grass field and a sing that reads, "Keep Off the Grass!" Once you arrive at the part of the story where you are describing the park you say, "And here's a park . . . and here's big field of grass . . . and here's a sign that says, Keep Off the Grass." As you hold your hand out for the children to see more closely you ask, "Where's the grass?" When they reach to point to the grassy area on your hand, you jerk your hand away and say, "Keep off the grass!"

Bev: *Often, while I am telling this story children will say, "If you live there, I think I live over here" pointing to a different part of my palm. Some may ask "Which grocery store is it?" or say "We don't shop there, we shop at_____!" Once when indicating where I live on my palm a child said, "My Daddy likes Boston. I think it's way over here" pointing to an area way up my forearm!*

Besides the fun in doing this finger-play with children, I can see how it helps many of them enter into the stage where they begin look at things in symbolic ways. A spot on my hand can represent something real to them -- such as their home or school. For children to follow along on this tour through their world while never leaving my hand leaves me speechless!

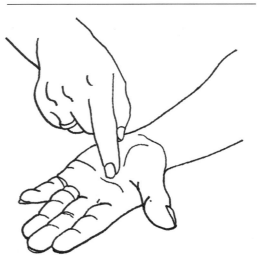

linden tree

Little Boy, Little Girl -

Little boy, little girl,	Yes, maam,
Did you go to the barn?	Yes, maam,
Did you feed my turkey?	Yes, maam,
Did you get any eggs?	Yes, maam,
Did you bring them home?	Yes, maam,
Did you give them to your Momma?	Yes, maam,
Did she put them in the bread?	Yes, maam,
Did she give you some?	Yes, maam,
Well, is the turkey's gone?	Yes, maam,
Which way did they go?	So, so
Which way did they go?	So, so
Will you help to find them?	Yes, maam,
Get ready, let's go!	Yes, maam,
Shoo, turkey, shoo shoo! (four times)	Shoo, turkey, shoo shoo!

Children pointing to where they went.

Little boy, little girl,	Yes, maam,
Did you go downtown?	Yes, maam,
Did you buy any eggs?	Yes, maam,
Did you bring them home?	Yes, maam,
Did you give them to your Momma?	Yes, maam,
Did she put them in the bread?	Yes, maam,
Did the turkeys go?	Yes, maam,
Which way did they go?	So, so
Which way did they go?	So, so
Will you help me to find them?	Yes, maam,
Get ready, let's go!	Yes, maam,
Shoo, turkey, shoo shoo! (four times)	Shoo, turkey, shoo shoo!

redwood

Mr. Brown and Mr. Black -

sycamore

The story of Mr. Brown and Mr. Black begins with an introduction of the characters.

Here is Mr. Brown inside his cozy home.

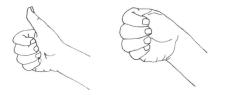

To introduce Mr. Brown, hold a closed hand out in front of you with your thumb up. Open fingers, fold thumb (Mr. Brown) down into your palm and close your fingers around him.

Here is Mr. Black inside his cozy home.

Repeat introduction for Mr. Black with other hand.

One day, Mr. Brown opens the door of his house, goes outside, and closes the door.

Open fingers -- lift up thumb -- close fingers.

Mr. Brown says, "Oh, what a lovely day! I think I'll go visit my friend, Mr. Black." So, he goes up the hill and down the hill, and up the hill and down the hill, and up the hill and down the hill, until he gets to Mr. Black's house.

Mr. Brown knocks on the door of Mr. Black. But no one answers. So, he knocks again. Nobody comes to the door. He hollers really loud. Then and he rang the bell But still nobody came and Mr. Brown went back home.

He goes down the hill and up the hill, and down the hill and up the hill . . . until he gets back home.

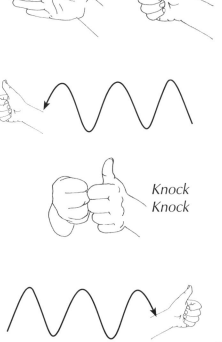

Knock
Knock

He opens the door, goes into his house and closes the door.

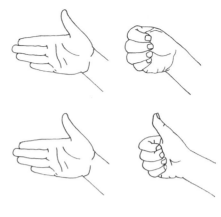

One day, Mr. Black opens the door of his house, goes outside, and closes the door.

Mr. Black says, "Oh, what a lovely day! I think I'll go visit my friend, Mr. Brown." So, he goes up the hill and down the hill, and up the hill and down the hill, and up the hill and down the hill, until he gets to Mr. Brown's house.

Mr. Black knocks on the door of Mr. Brown. But no one answers. So, he knocks again. Nobody comes to the door. He hollers really loud. Then and he rang the bell But still nobody came and Mr. Black went back home.

Knock
Knock

He goes down the hill and up the hill, and down the hill and up the hill . . . until he gets back home.

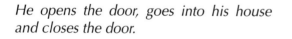

He opens the door, goes into his house and closes the door.

The next day, they both come out of their houses. The shut the door. And both of them say, "Oh, what a lovely day. I think I'll go visit my friend." And so . . .

. . . they go up the hill and down the hill until they meet at the top of the hill.

And Mr. Brown said to Mr. Black, "Hello, how are you?" And Mr. Black replied, "Oh, I'm fine, and how are you?" Mr. Brown answered, "I'm fine, too." And then they both went home. They went down the hill and up the hill and down the hill and up the hill and down the hill and up the hill until they got home.

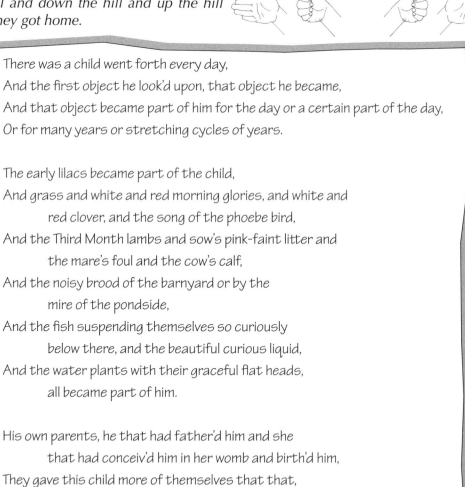

There was a child went forth every day,

And the first object he look'd upon, that object he became,

And that object became part of him for the day or a certain part of the day,

Or for many years or stretching cycles of years.

The early lilacs became part of the child,

And grass and white and red morning glories, and white and

   red clover, and the song of the phoebe bird,

And the Third Month lambs and sow's pink-faint litter and

   the mare's foul and the cow's calf,

And the noisy brood of the barnyard or by the

   mire of the pondside,

And the fish suspending themselves so curiously

   below there, and the beautiful curious liquid,

And the water plants with their graceful flat heads,

   all became part of him.

His own parents, he that had father'd him and she

   that had conceiv'd him in her womb and birth'd him,

They gave this child more of themselves that that,

The gave him afterward ever day, they became part of him.

             -- Walt Whitman

The Mushroom Chant -

mountain ash

Mush - - - - - - room,   mush - - - - - - room,

Cheese and crackers,   cheese and crackers,

Cup of chicken soup,   cup of chicken soup.

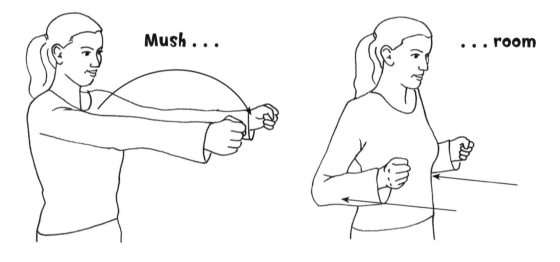

Mush . . .   **. . . room**

A fun and easy round you can do with children of all ages. The arms movements help everyone stay pretty much together. Also, this chant can easily be changed by letting the children pick the foods -- or whatever they wish to include in the chant.

Michael: *With the older kids this chant provides a little more of a challenge in the choosing of new words. They seem to want to pay more attention to the detail of timing -- how all three parts fit together -- and how it all sounds. For a chant that lends itself to "fiddling around with" it's hard to beat this one. And, if you also work with older children, it's a great opportunity to broach the subject of what half-notes, quarter notes and eighth notes are.*

Oh, Johnny -

(Adult part)
Oh, Johnny, oh, Johnny,
Will you wash your face, face, face?
Oh, Johnny, oh, Johnny,
Will you wash your face, face, face?

(Child's response)
Speak a little louder Mom,
I really cannot hear you.
(Repeat as many times as you like. The
adult lines a little louder each time).

(Adult whispers)
Oh, Johnny, oh, Johnny,
Would you like an ice cream cone?

(Child says in a loud voice)
Yes, Mother, yes, Mother,
I would like an ice cream cone!

white cedar

" . . . will you wash your face, face, face?"

One Potato, Two Potato -

One potato, two potato,

Three potato, four,

Five potato, six potato,

Seven potato, more.

When we do this traditional chant we start alternately pounding fists together. At that point we ask the kids, "Where else could we do it?" Their answers usually involve the top of the head, on the tummy, on your bum, on your knee, foot, tongue, toes, even "in the air" has been suggested.

Polly Put the Kettle On -

Polly put the kettle on,

Polly put the kettle on,

Polly put the kettle on,

We'll all have tea.

Suki take it off again,

Suki take it off again,

Suki take it off again,

They've all gone away.

Bev: *As we were gathering material for this book, I was talking to Cheryl, a long-time teacher at our school. I asked her if I could share something I watched her do. She brought the small wooden stove down from the loft and as she chanted, "Polly put the kettle on, Polly put the kettle on, Suki take it off again, we'll all have tea." The kids took turns taking the kettle off and putting it back on again. They were giggling and running back and forth and having the best fun. When I reminded Cheryl of this story she said she could hardly remember this. This, so often, happens to me. I fall in love with a chant, a rhyme or story and then get tired of it and set it aside. There is such a fine line between knowing the old "stuff" and keeping it going and staying fresh and alive with a new rhyme or chant. I hope this book is a combination of both . . . reminders and new.*

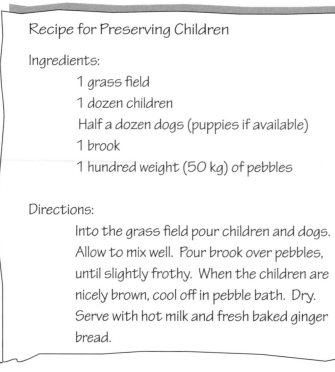

Recipe for Preserving Children

Ingredients:

       1 grass field

       1 dozen children

       Half a dozen dogs (puppies if available)

       1 brook

       1 hundred weight (50 kg) of pebbles

Directions:

       Into the grass field pour children and dogs. Allow to mix well. Pour brook over pebbles, until slightly frothy. When the children are nicely brown, cool off in pebble bath. Dry. Serve with hot milk and fresh baked ginger bread.

eastern
hemlock

Purple Stew Chant -

Making a purple stew, (Whip, whip -- whip, whip)

Making a purple stew (Scoobie doobie doo)

Purple potatoes, purple tomtoes,

Now you can do it, too.

tulip tree

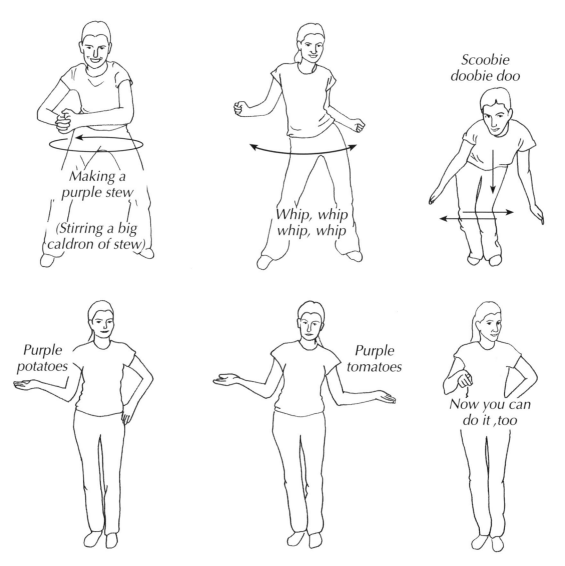

Making a
purple stew

(Stirring a big
caldron of stew)

Whip, whip
whip, whip

Scoobie
doobie doo

Purple
potatoes

Purple
tomatoes

Now you can
do it ,too

Ram Sam Sam -

A ram, sam, sam,

A ram, sam, sam,

Guli, guli, guli, guli, guli,

Ram, sam, sam,

A raffi, a raffi,

Guli, guli, guli, guli, guli,

Ram, sam, sam.

Pound your fists on each syllable of Ram Sam Sam. Roll your hands for Guli, Guli and form a circle overhead with your arms for Rafi.

After a couple times through this chant we continue to do the hand motions but we leave off one set of words, either ram, sam, sam or guli, guli or raffi. Ultimately, someone will suggest we do the whole chant with no words and just hand motions.

Recently we have extended this chant by doing the hand motions as small as we can using just our pinky fingers and then as big as we can with exaggerated hand motions. We have done it with two people working together -- one hand each. And, we've even used our feet instead of our hands or one foot and one hand.

A ram, sam, sam,

A ram, sam, sam,

Guli, guli, guli, guli, guli,

Ram, sam, sam,

A raffi, a raffi,

Guli, guli, guli, guli, guli,

Ram, sam, sam,

The Roly Poly Caterpillar -

cottonwood

The roly poly caterpillar,
Into the corner crept,
Wrapped a blanket 'round himself,
And then he soundly slept.
The roly poly caterpillar,
Awakened, by and by,
Spread his wings and found that he'd,
Become a butterfly.

The roly poly caterpillar,   *Into the corner crept,*   *Wrapped a blanket 'round himself, and*

Then he soundly slept,   *The roly poly caterpillar,*   *Awakened, by and by*

*Spread his wings
And found that he'd . . .*   *. . . become a butterfly.*

'Round and 'Round the Garden -

'Round and 'round the garden,

Like a Teddy Bear,

One step, two steps,

Tickle you under there.

elm

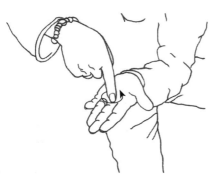

*'Round and 'round the garden,
like a teddy bear,*

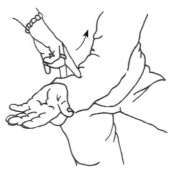

One step, two steps . . .

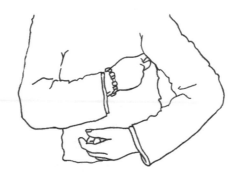

Tickle you under there!

---

*Draw a small circle with your finger in the middle of the child's hand while you say,
"'Round and 'round the garden, like a teddy bear." Walk fingers up arm during, "One
step, two steps" and you'll know what to do with the last line.*

'Round the World Chant -

Round the world, 'round the world,

To catch a big bear,

Where you gonna catch him?

Right in there!

apple

'Round the world, 'round the world
to catch a big ___?___ . . .

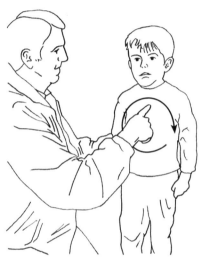 

'Round the world, 'round the world
to catch a big bear,

Where you gonna catch him?
Right in there!

For years we have noticed that children coming to our preschool have had no experience with fingerplays, nursery rhymes and/or the kind of "told" stories that have typically been associated with the childhood years. We now know there is real value to these simple, unsophisticated games between adult and child. And, we are increasingly aware of the danger of replacing those intimate moments with the counterfeit stimulation of TV and other forms of electronic media. In the words of Joseph Chilton Pearce: "Television floods the infant-child brain with images at the very time his or her brain is supposed to learn to make images from within. Storytelling feeds into the infant-child a stimulus that brings about a response of image making that involves every aspect of our triune system. Television feeds both stimulus and response and . . . few, if any, symbolic structures develop."

Sammy Put the Paper on the Wall -

hackberry

When Sammy put the paper on the wall,

He put the parlor paper in the hall,

Then he papered up the stairs,

He papered all the chairs,

He even put a border on grandma's shawl!

When Sammy put the paper on the wall,

He poured a pot of paste upon us all,

And now we're all stuck together,

Like birds of a feather,

Since Sammy put the paper on the wall.   (continued on next page)

In the past we have extended this chant by expanding on the story. After the first time through, we add that when Sammy gets up in the morning, he has a great big breakfast. Occasionally, the children will talk about what he probably ate. After the big breakfast, Sammy gets to work with lots of energy, so he goes really fast. When we get to the line, "he even put a border on grandma's shawl" we slow down, yawn and suggests, "Sammy can't go that fast all day. So, in the afternoon, he gets kind of tired and works real slow the rest of the day." And we continue the chant from there talking and moving in slow motion. Sometimes we add that "sometimes Sammy is real quite when he comes to work so all day long he works without a sound, like this" and we do the hand motions without saying the words.

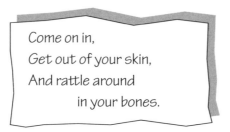

Come on in,
Get out of your skin,
And rattle around
        in your bones.

When Sammy put the paper on the wall,

He put the parlor paper in the hall,

Then he papered up the stairs,

He papered all the chairs,

He even put a border . . .

. . . on grandma's shawl!

When Sammy put the paper on the wall,

He poured a pot of paste upon us all,

And now we're all . . .

. . . stuck together,

Like birds of a feather,

Since Sammy put the paper on the wall,

Shoveling Chant -

Michael: *This chant happened during a car trip between Seattle and Portland. Bev and I wanted to create a chant that reflected the kind of play that occurs all the time at the Roseville Community Preschool. The kids provided their own hand motions and were also responsible for a few suggestions that made their way into this version.*

First you take a shovel and you stick it in the ground,
Then you take your foot and you push it on down,
      We're shovelin' ——— we're shovelin'
        Shovel, shovel, shovel, shovel, shovelin' (repeat last two lines)
You scoop to the left and you scoop to the right,
You scoop out the middle 'till the hole's just right,
      We're scoopin' ——— we're scoopin'
        Scoop, scoop, scoop, scoop, scoopin' (repeat)
Then you get a hose and you fill it to the brim,
Then you hold your nose and you jump on in,
      We're swimmin'– we're swimmin'
        Swim, swim, swim, swim, swimmin' (repeat)
We swim all day 'till the sun goes down,
When it's too cold to play we shiver all around,
      We're shiverin'——— we're shiverin'
        Shiver, shiver, shiver, shiver, shiverin' (repeat)
We call for Mom and she comes real fast,
She takes us upstairs and throws us in the bath,
      We're scrubbin' —— we're scrubbin'
        Scrub, scrub, scrub, scrub, scrubbin' (repeat)
We dry our body and we dry our head,
We put on pajamas and we jump in bed,
      We're sleepin' —— we're sleepin,'
        Sleep, sleep, sleep, sleep, sleepin.'
      And dreamin' ——— we're dreamin.'
        Dream, dream, dream, dream, dreamin,'
      'Bout shovelin' ———— shovelin,'
        Shovel, shovel, shovel, shovel, shovelin.'

joshua tree

Sleeping Bag Chant -

oak

Lying in my sleeping bag, couldn't fall asleep,

I looked at my watch and I wanted to weep,

I rolled the left and I rolled to the right,

And I heard every sound that you can hear at night,

And this is what I heard, I heard a cricket,

Ch ch ch chch, ch ch chch . . .

We usually start this chant by having the children pat their hands on their laps -- both hands in time or by alternating hands -- while we do the chant. When we get to the line "I rolled to the left and I rolled to the right" -- we roll hands in front of our body as we say the word "rooooolled" and then point to the left and to the right. On last line, we cup a hand to the ear as we say, "And I heard every sound you can hear at night." The children can add to the chant by responding to the question, "What do you hear night?" Below we have included the most recent incarnation of this wonderful chant.

I was lying in my sleeping bag, I couldn't get to sleep,

The wind began to blow, and the bugs began to creep,

So, I rolled the left, and I rolled to the right,

And, I heard every sound you can hear at night.

"What do you hear at night?"

Be prepared for a flood of responses to the question, "What do you hear at night?"
Crickets! -- which seems to be the definitive response from adults, in fact, that is how
Linnea Goode wrote the chant. Her chant also includes answers most young children
come up with, too, like "sirens, a dog barking." Children sometimes say a helicopter,
or people arguing, the refrigerator, the baby crying," . . . is there anyone who doesn't
remember how hard nighttime was as a child? A great opportunity to bring these things
out into the open.

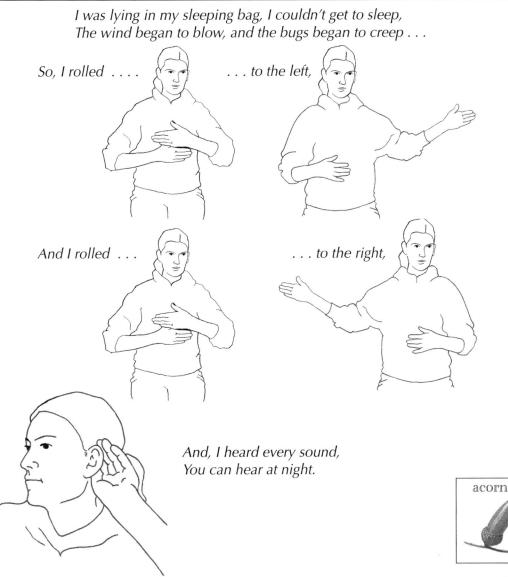

I was lying in my sleeping bag, I couldn't get to sleep,
The wind began to blow, and the bugs began to creep . . .

So, I rolled . . . . to the left,

And I rolled . . .   . . . to the right,

And, I heard every sound,
You can hear at night.

acorn

Soup, Soup -

A very simple chant that I heard Bessie Jones do. The refrain from the kids is, "Soup, soup." And, as the leader, you just say as many kinds of soup as you can think of. Most of the time the kids sound much like a train whistle's Toot Toot as throughout the chant and, for that matter, the rest of the day, whenever some says a type of soup within earshot of the kids, you can hear, "Soup, soup."

Chicken noodle,	Soup, soup!
Tomato,	Soup, soup!
Vegetable,	Soup, soup!
Minestrone,	Soup, soup!
Clam chowder,	Soup, soup!
Cream of broccoli,	Soup, soup!
Potato,	Soup, soup!
Cream of mushroom,	Soup, soup!

. . . .

To help get the chant off to a strong start we have found it's best to begin with Chicken Noodle and whenever possible make the other soups fit that number of syllables, like:

```
Chic - ken   noo - dle,
To   - ma    to  - oe,
Veg  - ta    ble - ul
```

Their was a little man,

Who had a little crumb,

And over the hill he did run, run, run,

With a belly full of fat,

And a big, tall hat,

And a pancake stuck to his

bum, bum, bum.

larch

There Was a Little Turtle - by Vachel Lindsay

There was a little turtle,

Who lived in a shell,

And he liked his home,

Very, very well.

He pokes his head out,

When he wants to eat,

And he pulls his head in,

When he wants to sleep.

The hand makes a pretty good turtle for chants like this. Just pull your thumb into your palm and wrap your fingers over it. When it's time for the turtle to eat, out pops the turtle's head, and when he wants to sleep, it slides back inside.

Bev: *Recently, I was reading the children's book titled, Hi, Harry by Martin Waddell. Harry is a turtle looking for a friend to play with. In the middle of reading the story to a group of children, I stopped and did this turtle chant. A few of the children watched me and some of the children spontaneously started making up their own fingerplay movements. Now, it has become kind of a tradition for me to stop and do the fingerplay before finishing the book. A great reminder to those who might be watching us that if it hasn't been in the hand it can't be in the brain. I've been saying this for nearly 30 years now and it is as true today as it has always been.*

Three-Corner Hat -

alder

My hat it has three corners,

Three corners has my hat,

And had it not three corners,

It would not be my hat.

Everytime through the chant leave off one of the words, but still act out the movements

1. My hat it has three corners, three corners has my hat, and had it not three corners, it would not be my hat

2. My_____ it has three corners . . .

3. My_____ it has_____ corners . . .

MY   HAT

THREE   CORNERS

Three Short-necked Buzzards -

Three short-necked buzzards,
(This line three times)
Sitting in a dead tree,

One flew away, what a shame.

Two short-necked buzzards, (2x)

Sitting in a dead tree,

One flew away, what a shame.

One short-necked buzzard, (1x)

Sitting in a dead tree,

One flew away, what a shame.

No short-necked buzzards,

Sitting in a dead tree,

One returned, we rejoice.

One short-necked buzzard,(1x)

Sitting in a dead tree,

One returned, we rejoice.

Two short-necked buzzards, (2x)

Sitting in a dead tree,

One returned, we rejoice.

Three short-necked buzzards (3x) . . . sitting in a dead tree.

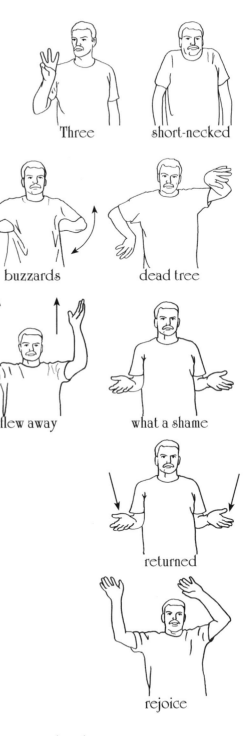

Three   short-necked

buzzards   dead tree

flew away   what a shame

returned

rejoice

To Stop the Train -

holly

To stop the train,

In cases of emergency,

Pull on the cord, pull on the cord,

Penalty for improper use,

Five pounds.

This chant comes from an actual sign that used to be posted in train cars in Great Britain warning riders that the cord was for emergencies ONLY! It can be done as a round with older children and adults. With the preschoolers, we all do it together and act out the words. For variety, we sometimes start quietly and get louder as we get toward the middle of the chant and then grow quieter as we near the end -- much like a train would sound as it approached and passed by.

To stop...

...the train,

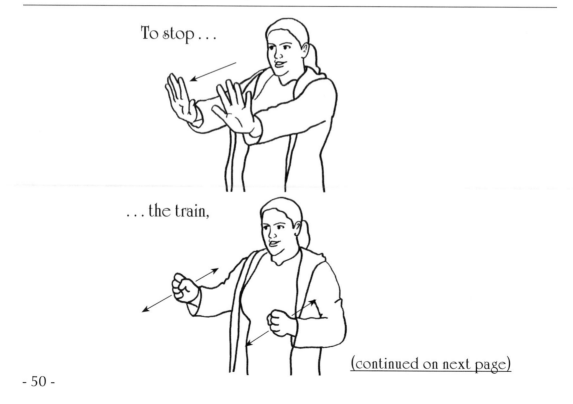

(continued on next page)

in cases of emergency . . .

Pull on the . . .   . . . cord.

Pull on the . . .   . . . cord,

Penalty for
improper use . . .

. . . five . . .

. . . pounds!

Turn the Page -

If I had the wings of an airplane,	[Turn the page, turn the page]
Up in the air I would fly,	[Turn the page, turn the page]
There I would stay as an airplane,	[Turn the page, turn the page]
Until the day that I die.	[Turn the page, turn the page]
Ooh la la, ooh la la, ooh la la la,	[Turn the page, turn the page]
Ooh la la, ooh la la la,	[Turn the page, turn the page]
Ooh la la, ooh la la, ooh la la la,	[Turn the page, turn the page]
Ooh la la, ooh la la la.	[Turn the page, turn the page]

Bev: *I started nearly 2,500 workshops over the course of dozen years with this chant. I would begin with, "Okay, everyone, take out your books." This usually caught everyone by surprise. They would look at each other and then blankly back up at me. I would then hold out my hands cupped together in front of me as if holding a small book. While gently swinging my "book" from side to side I would sing "If I had the wings of an airplane . . . up in the air I would fly . . ." Between lines I'd say "turn the page, turn the page" and turn a couple pages in my imaginary book. Occasionally someone was really baffled by my request and I would suggest they could look on with a friend. It has a beautiful melody and it's a great point of departure for talking about those moments we all had when a teacher would start the day with, "Take out your homework!"*

The Turtle in the Box -

butternut

There was a little turtle, and he lived in a box,

And he swam in the puddles, and he climbed on the rocks,

He snapped at the mosquito, he snapped at the flea,

He snapped at the minnow, and he snapped at me.

He caught the mosquito, he caught the flea,

He caught the minnow but he didn't catch me!

Two Little Blackbirds -

Two little blackbirds,

Sittin' on a hill,

One named Jack,

And the other named Jill,

Fly away Jack,

Fly away Jill,

Come back Jack,

Come back Jill.

This perfect little chant for little ones is another great example of the "going away, coming back" "now you see it, now you don't" "peek-a-boo" reality of young children.

Two little blackbirds,
sittin' on a hill,

One named Jack,

And the other named Jill,

Fly away Jack,

Fly away Jill,

Come back Jack,

Come back Jill.

Wake Up, Sleepy Head -

chestnut

The cows are lost. the cattle gone.

I think I'll rest 'till they come home,

I think I'll rest 'till they come home.

> Wake up, you sleepy heads, (spoken a little louder)
>
> And go and find the cattle!
>
> Wake up, you sleepy heads,
>
> And go and find the cows! (Repeat all)

On the lines, "I think I'll rest 'till they come home" everyone slowly drops down to rest on the ground (some kids will rest their head on a knee, others may lie all the way down) until someone yells, "Wake up, you sleepy heads . . ." and everyone jumps up.

Who Fed the Chickens? -

Who fed the chickens?   I did.

Who stacked the hay?   I did.

Who milked the cow?   I did.

On this fine day.

(Sing last line together).

The first time through the answer from the children is "I did." The next time we change the answer to "she did" while you find someone (a she) to point at. Then it's "he did" and "they did" and finally "we did."   When we do this in concerts, we have begun adding still more at the end of this chant. We just keep asking questions and the audience just keeps answering and pointing to questions like, "Well, who took out the garbage?" "Who made breakfast?" "Who fed the dog?" With each question you can hear a variety of "she dids" and "he dids" and "you did" -- it is really a lot of fun!

Yellow Butter, Purple Jelly, Red Jam, Black Bread -

Yellow butter, purple jelly, red jam, black bread,

Spread it thick and say it quick,

   [Yellow butter, purple jelly, red jam, black bread]

Yellow butter, purple jelly, red jam, black bread,

Spread it thicker, say it quicker,

   [Yellow butter, purple jelly, red jam, black bread]

Yellow butter, purple jelly, red jam, black bread,

Now repeat it, while you eat it.

   [Ymm bmm, pmm jmm . . .]

hawthorn fruit

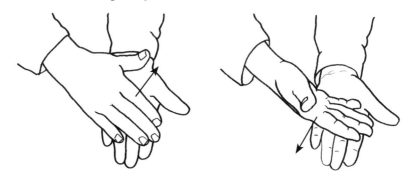

While you say the chant, hold one hand in front of you (palm up) and with the other hand pretend to spread the butter, jelly and jam on your "bread." With every time throught speed up as you go. We mumble the last line as if talking with a mouthful of food.

Morning has come,

   Night is away,

      Rise with the sun,

         And welcome the day.

Yes, Papa, Yes -

Now come on kids let's gather 'round,

    Yes, Papa, yes,

When your chores are done we'll go to town,

    Yes, Papa, yes,

Did you put out the cats and feed the dogs?

    Yes, Papa, yes,

Did you water the chickens and slop the hogs?

    Yes, Papa, yes,

Did you stuff the scarecrow full of hay?

    Yes, Papa, yes,

Did you let the ponies out to play?

    Yes, Papa, yes,

Did you chop the wood and stack it up?

    Yes, Papa, yes,

Did you help Old Blue with her pup?

    Yes, Papa, yes,

Did you get the horses all their oats?

    Yes, Papa, yes,

Did you give the cans to the billy goats?

    Yes, Papa, yes,

Well, I see you've got the work all done.

    Yes, Papa, yes,

Let's go to town and have some fun!

    Yes, Papa, yes!

Bev: *Here's a "call and response" chant I've done for many years with much success.*

loblolly

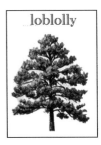

Towel & Hankie Folding

The Ballerina -

Using a large handkerchief, tie a simple knot in the middle of one of the four sides (*Fig.1*). With you hands grab opposite corners (*See* **A** *and* **B**, *Fig, 1*).

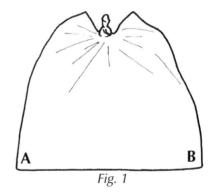

Fig. 1

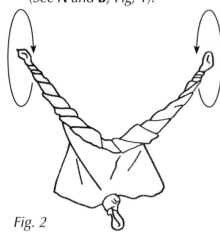

Fig. 2

. . . and as in Figure 2, begin "winding up the hankie by moving both hands simultaneously in small circles.

Once the hankie is wound up, quickly grasp the two corners in one hadn while pulling   u p on the knotted end (*Fig. 3*). Here is the ballerina!

To make her kick, while gently pulling apart with both hands, let one corner (foot) slip out of your grasp (*Fig. 4*).

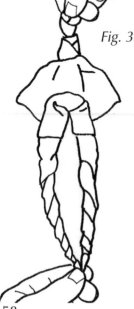

Fig. 3

Bev: *Once when showing this dancer to the kids, I noticed after winding that it wasn't quite as tight as I wanted. So, I said, "I think I'll just wind her head through her legs a couple times." One young boy said, "I hope you never do that*

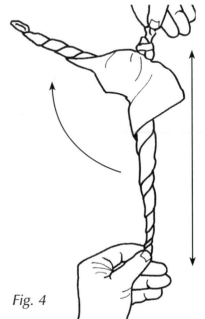

Fig. 4

Doll with Arms & Doll with a Hood -

Using a bar towel (*Figure 1*), roll evenly from each side until meeting in the center (*Figure 2*).

Fold rolls in half so that the rolls are to the inside of the fold (*Fig. 3*). Place a rubberband at fold (*Fig. 4*).

Turn doll over and pull rolls from behind out to the sides for form the "doll with arms" (*Fig. 5*). or

Push two of the rolls up and over the top where the rubberband is -- unrolling slightly as you go (*Fig. 6*).

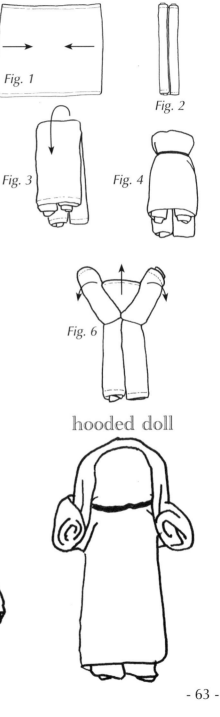

Fig. 1

Fig. 2

Fig. 3

Fig. 4

Fig. 6

We have found that bar towels work really well for these dolls. Feel free to experiment with all sorts and sizes of stuff, like large towels, blankets, and hankies.

You might want to put a hankie in your purse or car for emergency doll construction, like in a restaurant, on an airplane, at the grocery store . . .

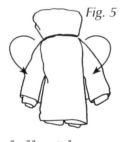

Fig. 5

doll with arms

hooded doll

Jacket Baby -

Fig. 1

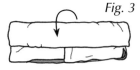

Fig. 2

Fig. 3

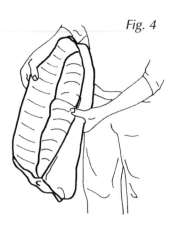

Fig. 4

Button or zip up the jacket (*Figure 1*).

Fold the arms across the front of the jacket (*Figure 2*).

Starting from the neck, tightly roll until you reach the bottom (*Fig. 3*).

Pull the bottom opening apart (*Fig. 4*) and turn inside-out around roll (*Fig. 5*).

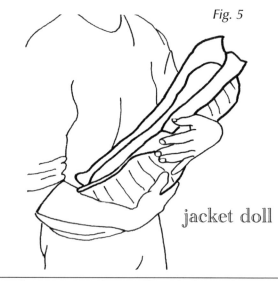

Fig. 5

jacket doll

Any jacket or sweatshirt will work for making this baby but we have found that jackets with thick linings make the best looking bundle -- especially if the lining of the jacket resembles a baby's blanket.

Michael: *Once before we performed a community concert, I made this jacket baby for a child that arrived early. When I looked up there was a growing line of kids waiting for their "jacket babies." There is something so special about homemade stuff like this. Things that can appear out of nowhere from any hankie, blanket or towel.*

The Sailboat -

Fold in half from the top down (*Figure 1 & 2*).

Fold the top corners down so that they meet in the middle along the bottom edge (*Figure 3 & 4*).

Next, fold up from the bottom a fold that is and inch or two wide. (*Fig. 4*).

While holding in both hands (see arrows Fig. 5) fold in half so that the part folded up from the bottom is still visible or on the outside of the fold (Fig 6).

Gather and hold with a rubber band the end or bow of the sailboat (Fig 7).

It's best to use a stiff handkerchief or bar towel or else the sail won't stand up.

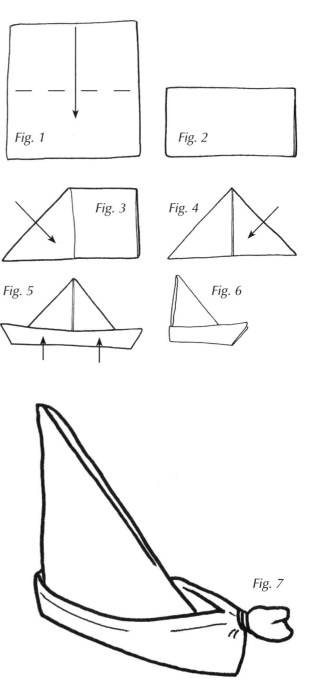

Fig. 1

Fig. 2

Fig. 3

Fig. 4

Fig. 5

Fig. 6

Fig. 7

The Turtle -

Gather and knot all four corners of a hankie (*Figure 1 & 2*).

Use knots to also form the head and tail (*Figure 3*).

Raise the middle of the hankie material to form the turtle's shell or place your hand underneath so that the back of your hand gives the shell its shape (*Fig. 4*).

Fig. 1   Fig. 2   Fig. 3

Fig. 4

The Little Bird Story -

Begin by folding a piece of paper in half. Fold to the bottom. *(Fig. 1)*

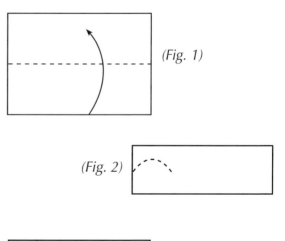

(Fig. 1)

Once there was a bird who went in search of a place that she could build a nest in which to lay her egg. She first flew over a small hill. *(With scissors, cut paper as indicated in Figure 2).*

(Fig. 2)

Unfortunately, there was no place for the bird to build her nest. So she continued flying and flew over a much larger hill. *(Cut shape of second hill. See Fig. 3)*

(Fig. 3)

But again the bird could not find a place to build her nest, so she kept flying on until she had flown over another hill much like the first hill. *(Cut as shown in Figure 4).*

(Fig. 4)

After flying over the third hill at last she spied a tree. In that tree she also saw a farmer's hat lodged in the branches. She examined the hat and thought maybe it might work as a nest. She turned it upside down, she cut off both ends and had made a proper nest from the old farmer's hat. *(See Fig. 5)*

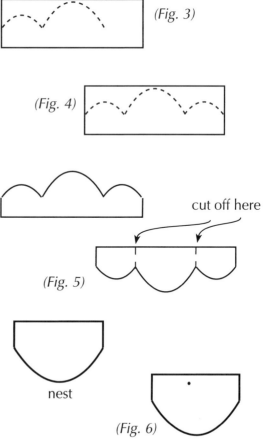

cut off here

(Fig. 5)

And in that hat she laid her egg. She sat on that egg for many days until one day the egg began to stir. She jumped off the egg and was surprised to find a small hole in her egg. *(With the end of the scissors, poke a small hole - See Fig. 6).*

nest

(Fig. 6)

As she watched as the egg started to crack.
It cracked and it cracked and it cracked.
*(With each crack - start cutting around the
hole -- (Fig 7).*

(Fig. 7)

crack!

crack!

crack!

(Fig. 8)

Finally, there was one last big CRACK!
*(Cut last as in Figure 9). Last cut should
be a small wedge cut out near the hole.*

(Fig. 9)

*(Unfold nest and refold in other direction
allowing the bird's head to rise. -- Fig.
10)*

(Fig.10)

The bird peeked over the edge of the nest
and up popped her new baby bird!

Little Paper Spinner

(Fig. 1)

Cut paper into 8 1/2″ x 1″ strips. At opposite
ends and on opposite sides, make two
small cuts halfway through the paper.
(Fig. 1)

(Fig. 2)

Bend the ends up towards each other
(without creasing) and insert the cuts into
each other. *(Fig. 2)*

(Fig. 3)

Hold sideways above your head and drop.
The paper will spin as it falls. (Fig. 3)

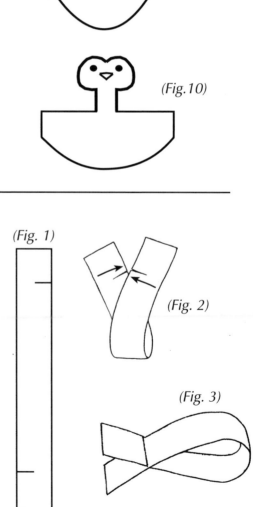

Little Bo Peep -

Fold a piece of card stock in hald lengthwise 3x5 or 4x6 inch. (*Fig. 1*) The bigger the sheep, the stiffer the paper must be.

Draw outline of sheep as in Figure 2.

Cut out along drawn line. To allow for ears, cut line between body and ear.

Unfold card, bend ears out slightly -- the sheep is ready to stand up.

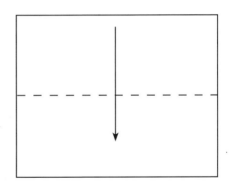

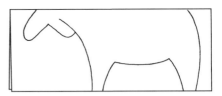

Little Bo Peep has lost her sheep,

And doesn't know where to find them,

Leave them alone, and they'll come home,

Dragging their tails behind them.

Paper Glider -

With a standard size sheet of paper 81/2 x 11 inches, crease corner to corner. *(Fig. 1)* Note: The folded paper should look like the example below. *(Fig. 2)*

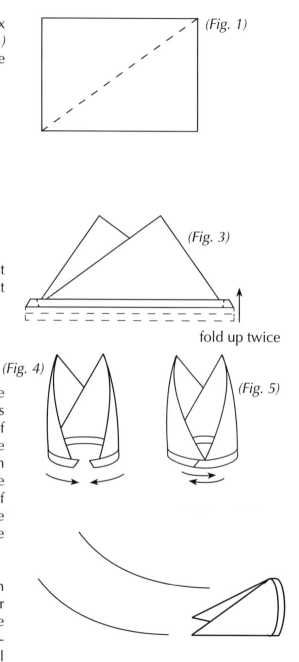

(Fig. 1)

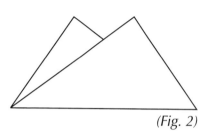

(Fig. 2)

Fold up from the bottom crease a fold that is approximately 1/2 inch wide. Repeat this fold.

(Fig. 3)

fold up twice

(Fig. 4)

(Fig. 5)

Once you have folded the bottom crease up twice, bring the ends around towards each other as in Figure 4. Slide one of the points inside the other. This make take some doing - but keep sliding them back and forth until one slips inside the other. You can apply tape to this spot if they don't seem to stay together. Once together, with you hands work the crease to make it as round as you can. *(Fig. 5)*

To launch the glider place your thumb in the notch at the end opposite the circular opening. Your thumb should be on the inside of the tube. Raise the glider over-head and in slow motion let your arm fall forward to release the glider.

Paper Helicopter -

To make this paper helicopter start by cutting a strip of paper 1½ x 8½ in. *(Fig. 1)*

(Fig. 1)

From one end, cut ⅓ of the way down the
middle of the strip of paper. (Dotted line
in Fig. 2)

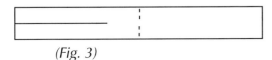

(Fig. 2)

Next, cut from each side a cut that goes ⅓
of the way through the strip of paper.
(Dotted lines in Fig. 3) Note: be careful
not to cut all the way through the strip.

(Fig. 3)

Fold the strips the form the helicopter's
rotor blades in opposite directions. Fold
in from one side along the bottom edge
and then fold over the first fold with the
paper on the other bottom side *(Fig. 4)*

*Hold as shown in illustration above to
launch. Make sure the blades are in a "V"
and not horizontal when you drop it.*

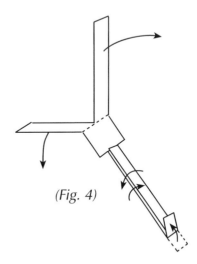

(Fig. 4)

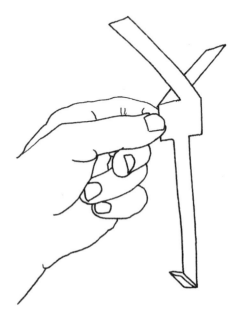

Ring-a-Round the Rosie -

Using a large piece of paper (news-paper-full size) and fold it in half. (*Fig. 1*).

Fold in half again. (*Fig. 2*)

Take bottom right corner up to left edge folding along dashed line. (*Fig. 3*)   Flip paper over, horizontally. (*Fig. 4 & 5*)

Fold over from right to left. (Fig. 6)

Draw outline of figure (one half, only shown as dased line. Note: lines that form the hands and feet go right off the side and the end of the paper). (Fig. 7)

Cut along drawn line and then unfold paper to show ring of figures.

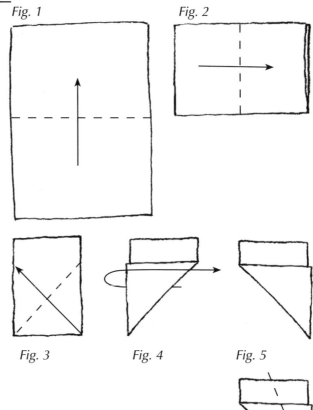

Fig. 1

Fig. 2

Fig. 3

Fig. 4

Fig. 5

Fig. 6

Fig. 7

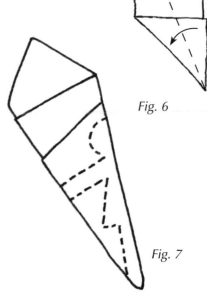

The Sailor and the Boat -

Once there was a young child who wanted to be a sailor. She asked her parents if they knew how to build a boat. They told her she would have to first build a shop. So, the firl began gathering lumber of all shapes and sizes with which to build her shop.

Fold paper in half and then in half again as in Figures 1 and 2.

Re-open second fold. (Fig. 3)

Using the center crease as a guide, fold the top corners toward the center -- where they meet. (Fig 4)

When at last the work on her shop was done, she stood back and to admired her work. *(Fig. 5)*

Before starting work on her boat, the young girl fashioned for herself a proper sailor hat. *Fold bottom tabs up and crease along edge of turned-down corners. (Fig. 6) Tabs get folded up on opposite sides. To complete hat, fold small corners tabs over, too. (Fig. 7)*

Now it was time to finish her boat. (The tab that was just turned up now gets turned up again. Start at on end (see arrows) and just keep folding up --both side at the same time. It will look like you are destroying the boat but keep going until you reach the opposite end then crease the upturned portion flat.

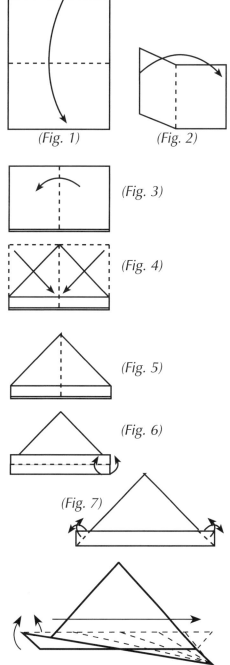

(Fig. 1)   (Fig. 2)

(Fig. 3)

(Fig. 4)

(Fig. 5)

(Fig. 6)

(Fig. 7)

When completed the boat should look something like illustration at right.

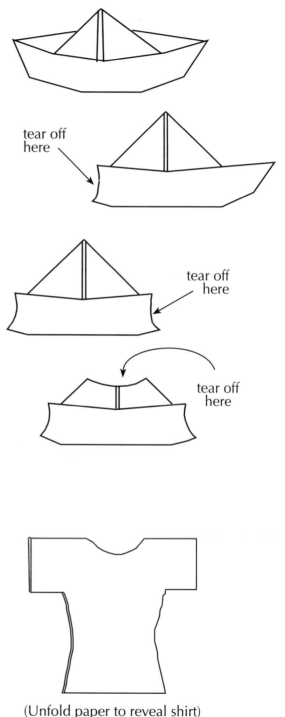

When at last her boat was finished, she launched it and sailed away on the deep, blue sea. As she sailed the wind began to blow and the waves grew to the size of mountains. But the girl sailed on. Without warning, an enormous wave came crashing down on the end of the girl's boat. (Tear off one end of the boat and discard).

tear off here

The girl ran to the other end of the boat and bravely sailed on. Soon after, another wave even bigger than the last came crashing down on the other end of the boat. (Tear off the other end of the boat).

tear off here

The girl ran to the top of the boat and bravely sailed on. And then, the largest wave to ever roll across the great ocean came thundering down on the little boat. CRASH! (Tear off the top to the boat).

tear off here

And in no time at all, the little boat sunk. At the very last second, the girl jumped into the stormy waters and swam for her-life. On the horizon she spied a Coast Gaurd ship that had come to resue her. After pulling her aboard the crew asked what had happened. She told them his sad tale and how he had lost everything he owned when the little boat went down The Coast Guard captain said, "Don't feel bad. At least you still have the shirt on your back!"

_____

(For a longer version, see the Captain From Krakow, A. Pellowski, <u>Family Story-telling Handbook</u>).

(Unfold paper to reveal shirt)

The Tall Sisters and the Shorter Sisters -
(or the Paper Box)

Michael: *I have told the Story of the Tall Sisters and the Shorter Sisters story many, many times over the years. I've seen version of the same story as "The Brother Short and the Brothers Long" in the book, <u>The Family Story-telling Handbook</u>, by Anne Pellowski. I've also used this paper folding techinique for making a box and a box with a top without using the accompanying story. If you do it with young children that may not be able to fold the story as you tell it, you will want to have made enough for everyone to have a box when the story ends -- because I guarantee you, every child will want one.*

This is the story of the Tall Sisters *(Fig. 1)* and the Shorter Sisters. *(Fig. 2)*

(Fig. 1)

(Fig. 2)

One day the Tall Sisters (fold paper in half lengthwise to indicate "tall" *(Fig. 3)* found an invitation in their mailbox. (Show folded paper - *Fig. 4)*

(Fig. 3)

(Fig. 4)

They opened the invitation and it read, "You are both invited to come to the Center tonight for a party." And so they went. One Tall Sister went to the Center and the other Tall Sister went to the Center. *(Fig. 6)*

(Fig. 5)

(Fig. 6)

When they arrived at the Center they walked up the front doors *(Fig. 7)* and they opened the doors and went inside.*(Fig. 8)*

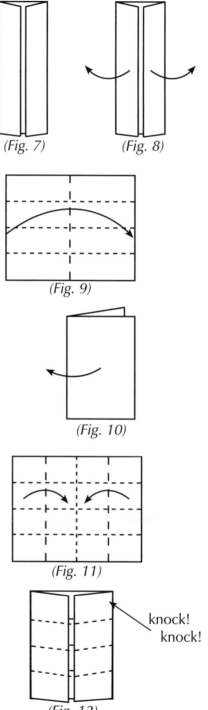

(Fig. 7)   (Fig. 8)

Rotate paper sideways as in (Fig. 9) and fold in half.

That very same day on the other side of town, the Shorter Sisters (fold paper in half to indicate "shorter") also found an invitation in their mailbox.

(Fig. 9)

They opened the invitation *(Fig. 10)* and it read, "You are both invited to come to the Center tonight for a party." And so they went.

(Fig. 10)

One Shorter Sister went to the Center and then the other Shorter Sister went to the party. (Fig 10). And when the arrived at the Center they found a set of doors (Fig. 11) They tried to open the doors but they were locked!

(Fig. 11)

One Shorter Sister decided to knock on the door. So she rapped on the corner of the door but nobody came. So she rapped really hard!

knock!
knock!

(Fig. 12)

She rapped so hard that the door broke! (Fold down the corner as shown. *(Fig 13)* The other Shorter Sister rapped on the door, and when nobody answered, she rapped really hard. And the door broke on the other side, too! (Fig. 13).

Then, both Shorter Sisters began kicking the door -- one kicking on one side and the other kicking on the other side. The door broke on both sides! *(Fig. 15)* It was then that they noticed a small crack between the two doors. *(arrow -- Fig. 16)*

Working together they pushed on the crack to see if they could make it a bit bigger. (Fold back one flap from the center so that if lies over the turned down corners. *Fig. 17)* It worked! The door opened ust a crack. So, they tried to make the crack even bigger by pushing on the other side and that worked as well. *(Repeat on other side -- Fig. 18)*

And now, they found they could each place the fingers of a their hand in the crack they had created. While they gently began pulling, the doors open. (Fig 19).

Once you have pulled the paper open, begin creasing each of the four corners. *(Fig. 20)* As the door opened all the way, the Shorter Sisters walked into the Center. Overhead they saw a sign that read, "We've been waiting for you to come to this place!"

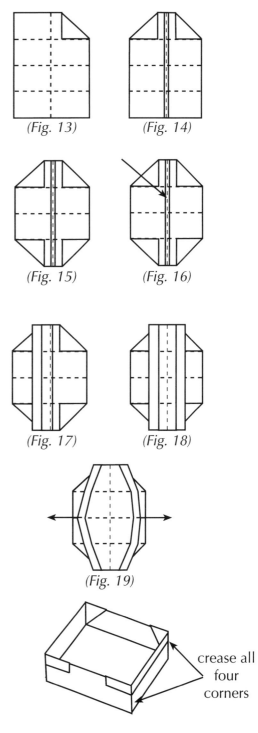

(Fig. 13)　　(Fig. 14)

(Fig. 15)　　(Fig. 16)

(Fig. 17)　　(Fig. 18)

(Fig. 19)

crease all four corners

Umbrella -

Use a piece of paper 8½ x 11 inches to make the umbrella. Start by folding the paper in half lengthwise. Draw the shape as shown in illustration at right.

Once you have done this a few times it becomes easy to do without having to draw it first.

We chant the following poem as I cut out the shape -- opening it up when completed to show the umbrella.

The kids will pick up the poem after a few times through and some join in. Others may offer ideas about where else the rain could fall, "on the sidewalk" " on my house" "on the school" "on the . . ."

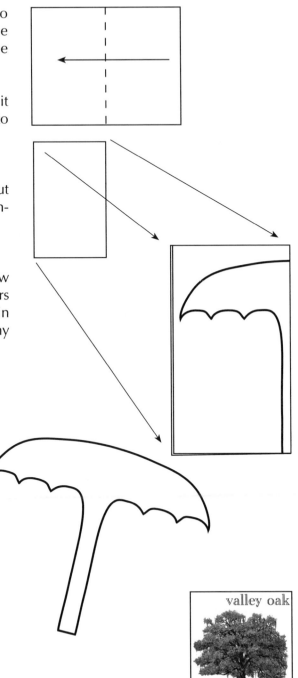

Rain on the green grass,

And rain on the tree,

Rain on the house-top,

But not on me. (Repeat)

Why not?

Because I have an umbrella!

valley oak

The Ordinary Man

Once in an ordinary town there lived an ordinary man named John. He had an ordinary wife whose name was Mary. And they had two ordinary children named, Joe and Jane.

Everyday, John would wake up, put on his ordinary clothes and go downstairs to eat his ordinary everyday breakfast. When he was finished eating he would say goodbye to his ordinary wife and children and walk from his ordinary home to where he worked, doing his very ordinary job. As he walked to work his path would take past the town's cemetery. As he walked by the cemetery the wind would blow (Whoosh) and the leaves would rattle (Scritchety scritch scritch).

At the end of a long ordinary day of work and when it was time to walk home, sometimes it was very dark. And John would walk home taking his ordinary route home past the cemetery. And in the darkness John would hear the wind blow (Whoosh) and the leaves rattle (Scritchety scritch scritch) and as he got closer and closer to the cemetery he heard a voice saying, "Turn me over, turn me over."

This scared John very much and he would run home just as fast as he could. When he got home he would tell his wife what happen. Mary would say, "But, John, you're just an ordinary man and we're an ordinary family. Things like this just don't happen to ordinary people." Nothing John said could convince her that his story was true. So, after an ordinary dinner they would all go to sleep at the end of a another very ordinary day.

The next day, John woke up, put on his ordinary clothes and went downstairs to eat his ordinary everyday breakfast. When he was finished eating he said goodbye to his ordinary wife and children and walk from his ordinary home to his very ordinary job. As he walked by the cemetery the wind blew (Whoosh) and the leaves rattled (Scritchety scritch scritch).

At the end of a another ordinary long day of work and it was time to walk home, it was very dark -- even darker than the night before. And John walked home taking his ordinary route home past the cemetery. And in the darkness John heard the wind blow (Whoosh) and the leaves rattle (Scritchety scritch scritch) and as he got closer and closer to the cemetery he heard a voice saying, "Turn me over, turn me over."

Just like the night before, this scared John very much and ran home just as fast as he could. When he got home he told his wife what happen and Mary said, "But, John, you're just an ordinary man and we're an ordinary family. Things like this just don't happen to ordinary people." Nothing John said could convince her that his story was true. So, after another ordinary dinner they all went to sleep at the end of a another very ordinary day.

The next day, John woke up, and just like the day before and the day before that, he put on his ordinary clothes and went downstairs to eat his ordinary everyday breakfast. When he was finished eating he said goodbye to his ordinary wife and children and walk from his ordinary home to his very ordinary job. As he walked by the cemetery the wind blew (Whoosh) and the leaves rattled (Scritchety scritch scritch).

At the end of a another ordinary long day of work and it was time to walk home, it was very dark -- even darker than the night before and the night before that.   John walked home taking his ordinary route home past the cemetery. And in the darkness John heard the wind blow (Whoosh) and the leaves rattle (Scritchety scritch scritch) and as he got closer and closer to the cemetery he heard a voice saying, "Turn me over, turn me over."

When John heard this he said to himself, "Tonight, I'm not running home. I'm gonna find out what is making that noise." As he entered the cemetery he slowly walked toward the sound, "Turn me over, turn me over." He got closer and closer. "Turn me over, turn me over," he heard again.   As he walked over a very small hill in the cemetery where the sound was coming from, he heard, "Turn me over, turn me over," he saw a red and orange glow. The sound was getting louder as he got closer and the glow got bigger and bigger.

"Turn me over, turn me over." As John got really close to the red and orange glow he could see a grate -- like a barbecue grate. John looked really close and in the middle of that grate he saw a hamburger and that hamburger was saying, "Turn me over, turn me over."

The Ordinary Man shares with stories like Hairy Scary Monster and Long One Story an element that is common to many stories or folktales -- the fear of the unknown. Another frequently used element is a resolution that provides a reminder (or comfort) to children that things aren't as scary as they sometimes seem to be.

There are so many occasions during the telling of this story for the children to participate. Every time the word "ordinary" is mentioned there's going can be a discussion about ordinary names, ordinary foods, ordinary jobs, etc. Acting out with hand motions the wind blowing and the leaves rattling and the ordinary man running home helps to keep the story lively. I do love that when the children, who have heard this story, ask me to "tell him the hamburger story, he hasn't heard it, yet" they've given away the punchline.

After sharing this story at a conference of early childhood educators we heard back from one of them who had retold the story later that same evening. To a small group of "bikers," (which included her father) who had all gathered for Dollar Taco Night at a local bar, she told the story. They immediately insisted she retell it. They began callling people over to hear the story. And, as people continued to arrive, she would again and again be coaxed to "tell the Ordinary Man Story." What a wonderul reminder that a story told outloud is a pleasureable human experience for people of all ages.

The Hairy Scary Monster

In the Land of the Hairy Scary Monster there also lived a Momma Mouse with her four little ones. Momma Mouse worked very hard taking care of her family and their home. At the end of a very long day as Momma Mouse was making dinner she became very thirsty.

She said to the oldest of her little ones, "Please take the pail and go down to the creek and bring me a drink of water."

The oldest one said, "Momma, I don't want to go because I am afraid of the Hairy Scary Monster that lives in the cave!"

But Momma Mouse said, "I am really thirsty and I, really need some water. I know you will think of something."

The oldest mouse took the pail and tip-toed across the field toward the creek when he heard the Hairy Scary Monster yell, "I'm gonna come down there and get you right now!" The oldest mouse dropped the pail and ran and hid behind a tree.

After the longest time, the Momma Mouse said, "I wonder what is taking so long? I'm am still so thirsty." And she said to the second-oldest mouse. "Please take the pail and go down to the creek and bring me a drink of water."

The second-oldest mouse said, "Momma, I don't want to go because I am afraid of the Hairy Scary Monster that lives in the cave!"

But Momma Mouse said, "I am really thirsty and I, really need some water. I know you will think of something."

The second-oldest mouse ran as fast as she could across the field toward the creek when she hear the Hairy Scary Monster, yell, "I'm gonna come down there and get you right now!" The second-oldest mouse dropped the pail and ran and hid behind a tree.

When the second-oldest mouse to didn't come back, the Momma Mouse said to the third-oldest mouse, "Please take the pail and go down to the creek and bring me a drink of water."

The third-oldest mouse said, "Momma, I don't want to go because I am afraid of the Hairy Scary Monster that lives in the cave!"

But Momma Mouse said, "I am really thirsty and I, really need some water. I know you will think of something."

The third-oldest mouse took the pail and quietly crawled around the back of the cave and across the field toward the creek and just before he got there he heard the Hairy Scary Monster yell, "I'm gonna come down there and get you right now!" The third-oldest mouse dropped the pail and ran and hid behind a tree.

After a very long time, the Momma Mouse said to the tiniest mouse. "Please take the pail and go down to the creek and bring me a drink of water."

The tiniest mouse said, "Momma, I don't want to go because I am afraid of the Hairy Scary Monster that lives in the cave!"

But Momma Mouse said to the tiniest mouse, "I am really thirsty and I, really need some water. I know you will think of something."

The tiniest mouse took the pail and began to walk across the field toward the creek when she heard the Hairy Scary Monster, yell, "I'm gonna come down there and get you right now!" The tiniest mouse said, "Hairy Scary Monster, you are not the scariest thing there is and I am not afraid of you!" The Hairy Scary Monster, said, "There is nobody scarier than me, I am the scariest of all." The tiniest mouse said, "I'm sorry, but you are definitely not the scariest of all!"

The Hairy Scary Monster came out of his cave and demanded to know where the scariest monster lives.

The tiniest mouse, said, "He lives up in that very tree," pointing up a very tall tree. The Hairy Scary Monster began to climb the tree as the tiniest mouse watched and said, "It lives higher, higher . . . even higher!" As the monster climbs the tree, the little mouse ties the monster's long tail to the tree in many, many knots.

The tiniest mouse then took the pail down to the creek and scooped up a big, cool drink for her Momma. The other little ones followed her back home and as they past under the very tall tree the Hairy Scary Monster called down to them, "I can't get down, I can't get down. Don't leave me up here?"

The tiniest mouse said, "I know you will think of something." When they all got home, they gave their thirsty Momma Mouse her drink of water, and as they all sat down to dinner she said, "I knew you would think of something."

The confident reassurance that the mother bathes her children in and the courage that the "littlest ones" take from this story make it one of our favorites.

Leaving Home

There once lived a Momma Mouse and her many, many children. One day as she looked at her children she said, "You are all grown and must now go out and live on you own. But, before you go there is something you must know."

Find a good home.
Eat fine food.
Be kind to your friends.
And, DON'T LOOK BACK!

The leader of the story then has all the children gather into a line behind her and they meander along chanting, "Find a good home, eat fine food, be kind to your friends, and DON'T LOOK BACK!"

This story becomes an impromptu dance with Momma Mouse leading the little mice around the room as another adult clandestinely joins in the rear of the line and becomes the CAT. The children will not be able to resist looking back and one by one are captured by the cat. Some kids, when they know they're next, just go limp and fall in a heap to the ground -- laughing. We have yet to have a child that doesn't look back.

Leaving Home is a quick story that can be played over and over in a short period of time. It is also a reminder to adults that whenever we say, "Don't . . ." whatever it is we are referring to just became irresistible to the child.

The Story of Hans and Maria

Once upon a time, near a small village, there lived a man and his wife and their daughter named Maria. Maria had grown into a young lady and over the years had become very good friends with a villager; a young man named Hans.

Whenever she thought of Hans, she would say to herself, "Maybe, someday we might fall in love, we might get married, and we might even have a baby."

Maria decided to invite Hans over to her house so they could more spend time together. When Hans arrived, Maria took him into the house where the sat talking, holding hands and drinking apple cider. They talked and talked and were having a wonderful time when Maria noticed they had run out of apple cider. She said to Hans, "I see we are out of cider. I am going down in to the cellar where I can get some more for us to drink." And Maria walked to the top of the stairs, walked down the stairs, opened the door of the cellar and went in. As she reached for the apple cider, she saw, stuck in the ceiling of the cellar -- an axe! And she began to wail and sob.

Meanwhile, Maria's mother walked into the room where Hans sat waiting. She asked, "Hans, where is Maria?"

Hans replied, "She went down into the cellar to bring more apple cider and she has been down there for the longest time."

The mother said, "Well, I'll go down to the cellar and help her." And the Mother walked to the top of the stairs, walked down the stairs, opened the door of the cellar and went in. When she got there she saw Maria crying and sobbing and asked, "Maria, whatever is wrong?"

Maria cried, "Maybe, someday Hans and I might fall in love, we might get married, and we might even have a baby. And one day that baby could come down the cellar stairs, open the door, walk in to the cellar and that axe would go CHOP!" And Maria cried, "Waaahh!" The Mother cried, "Waaahh!" And, they both stood in the cellar crying and sobbing.

Meanwhile, the father came into the room where Hans sat waiting. He asked, "Hans, where is Maria?"

Hans replied, "She went down into the cellar to bring more apple cider and she has been down there for the longest time."
The Father said, "Well, I'll go down to the cellar and help her." And, the Father walked

to the top of the stairs, walked down the stairs, opened the door of the cellar and went in. When she got there she saw Maria and Mother crying and sobbing and asked, "Mother, whatever is wrong?"

Mother cried, "Maybe, someday Hans and Maria might fall in love, they might get married, and they might even have a baby. And one day that baby could come down the cellar stairs, open the door, walk in to the cellar and that axe would go CHOP!" And Maria cried, "Waaahh!" The Mother cried, "Waaahh!" And, the Father cried. And, they all stood in the cellar crying and sobbing.

Meanwhile, the family cat came into the room where Hans sat waiting. The cat looked around, not seeing anybody, asked, "Meow, meow meow meow?"

Hans shrugged and replied, "They all went down into the cellar to bring more apple cider and they have been down there for the longest time."

The cat walked to the top of the stairs, walked down the stairs, opened the door of the cellar and went in. When the cat got there and saw Maria and Mother and the Father crying and sobbing, the cat asked, "Meow, meow meow meow?"

And the Father said, "Well, someday Hans and Maria might fall in love, they might get married, and they might even have a baby. And one day that baby could come down the cellar stairs, open the door, walk in to the cellar and that axe would go CHOP!" And Maria cried, "Waaahh!" The Mother cried, "Waaahh!" And, the Father cried. And the cat cried, too. And, they all stood in the cellar crying and sobbing.

Finally, Hans grew tired of waiting and walked to the top of the stairs, walked down the stairs, opened the door of the cellar and went in. When he got there she saw Maria, the Mother, the Father and the cat crying and sobbing and asked, "Whatever is wrong?"

And the cat said, "Meow, meow meow meow meow . . . (recount the story using only the meowing sounds the cat would make).

At the end of the cat's story, Hans walked over to the axe and pulled it out of the ceiling, set on the table in the cellar and turned to walk out but before he left he said, "You people are crazy." And he left and nobody has seen him since.

This story of Hans and Maria is actually the first part of a much longer folktale. We have seen it under many different titles, the one we know is called the Three Sillies. The children love the CHOP! and, of course, the cat's part in this funny tale. It's also a great example of how stories have repeating parts that hold the story together and allow for the audience to be a part of the telling. Anytime you can involve the body and the mind in the story, it's a winner.

Here are some of the hand motions we use for this wonderful story.

The descending of the cellar stairs offers a great place to use an amusing sound during this story. We've been using a sort of rapid, "doodle, doodle, doodle, doodle . . ." as we walk our fingers down imaginary stairs.

We act out the part where Maria imagines "we might fall in love, we might get married and we might have a baby." Here she's falling in love with her hands to her heart.

. . . maybe getting married . . .

placing an imaginary ring
on her finger.

. . . we might have a baby!

And, of course,

CHOP!!!

The Sweet Patootie Doll

Once upon a time there as a little girl who lived in the country. There was woods nearby where she played sometimes. Her Mom and Dad were farmers and they grew lots of vegetables, fruit and grain. She didn't have any toys, but she had lots of places to dig in the dirt, and there were rocks, pieces of wood and places to build hideouts. But what she wanted more than anything else was a doll.

Her Mom and Dad could not afford to buy her a doll. Everyday the little girl asked her Mom and Dad for a doll and one day when her Dad was digging up the sweet potatoes, he found one that had eyes that looked just like real eyes and he gave it to his daughter, saying, "Here is the beginnings of a doll."

So, the little girl started collecting things to make her doll. She found scraps of material, bits of ribbon, string and buttons and she made herself a doll. She named her doll Sweet Patootie because it started from a sweet potato. She loved her and took the doll everywhere she went.

One day, as she went off into the woods to play, she lay the doll down on a tree stump. The little girl went off to play and played for hours and hours. Before she realized it, the forest started to grow dark and she quickly ran home, forgetting her Sweet Patootie doll. When she got home and climbed into bed, she suddenly remembered that she had left her Sweet Patootie doll on the tree stump in the forest but it was too dark for her to find her.

All night long the Sweet Patootie doll lay on the tree stump. In the dark, the Sweet Patootie doll heard a noise. It was a squirrel and the squirrel came up to the Sweet Patootie doll and sniffed her. The squirrel sniffed her head, and sniffed her eyes and sniffed her mouth. Sweet Patootie doll was frightened but she knew what she was for and it was not for eating.

A little while later a raccoon came up to the Sweet Patootie doll as she lay on the tree stump. The raccoon sniffed the Sweet Patootie doll and nudged it with its nose. The Sweet Patootie doll was frightened but she knew what she was for and it was not for eating.

Soon, a opossum wandered close to the tree stump where the Sweet Patootie doll lay. The opossum sniffed the Sweet Patootie doll and nudged her with its nose. The Sweet Patootie doll was frightened but she knew what she was for and it was not for eating. Finally, the sun came up. It was a new day. The Sweet Patootie doll was hoping that the little girl would come back looking for her and would find her. Then she heard a noise! At first, she was just sure it was another animal coming to pester her. She was frightened but then she saw that it was the little girl. She had come back and had found her in the forest on the tree stump we she had left her. The little girl picked her up and hug and kissed the Sweet Patootie doll. The Sweet Patootie doll smiled and thought to herself, "I know what I am for . . . and it's for loving."

The Candle Story

There once was a family that lived in the days before people had electricity. The only heat they had came from the fireplace. The only water they had came from the well. And the only light they had came from the candles they used when the sun went down. In this family there was a father, a mother, a big brother, a big sister and a little baby who couldn't walk, yet -- just crawl.

One evening after dinner when it was time for bed, the father lit a candle so the family could go upstairs to the bedrooms where they slept. They all followed their father as he walked up the stairs with the candle.

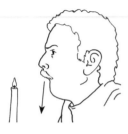

When they got to the top of stairs, the father said, "I'll blow out the candle." But when he blew, the candle didn't go out because the father blew like this.

The baby looked up at the father and said, "I can do it, I can do it." The father said, "Oh, you're too little."

The mother said, "Let me try." But when she blew, the candle didn't go out because the mother blew like this.

The baby looked up at the mother and said, "I can do it, I can do it." But, the mother said, "Oh, you're much too little."

Then the big brother said, "I think I can do it." But when he blew, the candle didn't go out because the big brother blew like this.

The baby looked up at his big brother and said, "I can do it, I can do it." But, the big brother said, "Oh, you're way too little."

So, then the big sister said, "Can I try? I think I can do it." But when she blew, the candle didn't go out because the big sister blew like this.

The baby looked up at his big sister and said, "I can do it, I can do it." But, the big sister said, "Oh, you're way, way too little."

They all wanted to go to bed but they couldn't leave the candle burning. So, they stood at the top of the stairs hoping somebody would come by and help them. When they heard a noise that sounded like someone walking past their house, they yelled, "Help, help!"

As luck would have it, it was a policeman. He ran up the stairs and blew the candle out. They all thanked him because now they could go to bed. But, the policeman said, "Wait a minute. How will I get back downstairs and out of this house without a light?"

The father said, "Oh, you're right. I know, I'll light the candle and you'll be able to see as you go back down the stairs." The policeman said, "Yes, that will work. Thank you." And when he got back downstairs, he stopped at the door, turned and said, "Good night," and then he left.

So, the family all stood at the top of stairs, when the father said, "I'll blow out the candle." But when he blew, the candle didn't go out because the father blew like this.

The baby looked up at the father and said, "I can do it, I can do it." The father said, "Oh, you're too little." The mother said, "Let me try." But when she blew, the candle didn't go out because the mother blew like this.

The baby looked up at the mother and said, "I can do it, I can do it." But, the mother said, "Oh, you're much too little." Then the big brother said, "I think I can do it." But when he blew, the candle didn't go out because the big brother blew like this.

The baby looked up at his big brother and said, "I can do it, I can do it." But, the big brother said, "Oh, you're way too little." So, then the big sister said, "Can I try? I think I can do it." But when she blew, the candle didn't go out because the big sister blew like this.

The baby looked up at his big sister and said, "I can do it, I can do it." But, the big sister said, "Oh, you're way, way too little."

So, they all stood at the top of the stairs wanting to go to bed but they couldn't leave the candle burning. They waited and waited hoping somebody would come by and help them. Then they heard a noise that sounded like someone walking past their house, they yelled, "Help, help!"

As luck would have it, it was the fireman. He ran up the stairs and blew the candle out. They all thanked him because now they could all go to bed. But, the fireman said, "Wait a minute. How will I get back downstairs and out of this house without a light?"

The father said, "Oh, you're right. I know, I'll light the candle and you'll be able to see as you go back down the stairs." The fireman said, "Yes, that will work. Thank you." And when he got back downstairs, he stopped at the door, turned and said, "Good night," and then he left.

So, the family all stood at the top of stairs, when the father said, "I'll blow out the candle." But when he blew, the candle didn't go out because the father blew like this.

The baby looked up at the father and said, "I can do it, I can do it." The father said, "Oh, you're too little." The mother said, "Let me try." But when she blew, the candle didn't go out because the mother blew like this.

The baby looked up at the mother and said, "I can do it, I can do it." But, the mother said, "Oh, you're much too little." Then the big brother said, "I think I can do it." But when he blew, the candle didn't go out because the big brother blew like this.
The baby looked up at his big brother and said, "I can do it, I can do it." But, the big brother said, "Oh, you're way too little." So, then the big sister said, "Can I try? I think I can do it." But when she blew, the candle didn't go out because the big sister blew like this.

The baby looked up at his big sister and said, "I can do it, I can do it." But, the big sister said, "Oh, you're way, way too little."

And so, for the third time, they all stood at the top of the stairs wanting to go to bed but they couldn't leave the candle burning.   They waited and waited hoping somebody would come by and help them.   Then they heard a noise that sounded like someone walking past their house, they yelled, "Help, help!"

As luck would have it, it was the baker going to work. He ran up the stairs and blew the candle out. They all thanked him because now they could all go to bed. But, the baker said, "Wait a minute. How will I get back downstairs and out of this house without a light?"

The father said, "Oh, you're right. I know, I'll light the candle and you'll be able to see as you go back down the stairs." The baker said, "Yes, that will work. Thank you." And when he got back downstairs, he stopped at the door, turned and said, "Good night," and then he left.

So, the family all stood at the top of stairs, when the father said, "We still need to blow out this candle so we can all go to bed." They all tried again to blow out the candle. The father blew like this, and the mother blew like this, and the big brother blew like this and the big sister blew like this. The baby looked up at all of them and said, "I can do it, I can do it." And they all said, "Okay, here, give it a try." And the baby went . . . TThhppptt!

And blew out the candle.

What's the Name of That Tree?

Once, long ago in the land where no rain fell and no grass grew, there was great hunger. All of the animals; the elephant, the monkey, the gazelle, the giraffe, the tortoise and all the rest were very, very hungry. They began to search for food but none of them could find anything to eat no matter where they looked.

The animals gathered to talk about how they could find food. They realized there was only one place left where they hadn't looked and that was on the other side of the great wide plain. So, all of the animals, except for the mighty lion -- the king of the jungle -- began the long walk across the great wide plain to look for food.

They walked and walked for many days until the giraffe noticed something on the horizon. They all looked at where she was pointing and, sure enough, there was something on the other side of the great wide plain. It was a tiny bump on the horizon and as they got closer, they could see that the bump was actually a tree. And not only that but it was a very tall tree, as well.

When they animals got to the tree they could see that the tree had fruit hanging from it's limbs. It was a fruit that none of them had ever seen before. It was a yellow as the ripest bananas, as purple as the purplest plums, green as any melon ever was, and red as the biggest pomegranate. Most of all, it smelled like all of the fruits put together.

Unfortunately, the tree was very tall, too. So tall that even the tallest giraffe couldn't reach the fruit, and the tree trunk was so smooth that even the monkey couldn't climb up it. The animals all cried because the fruit smelled so good and they were so very hungry, but no one could figure out how to get the fruit.

Just then, the wise, old tortoise spoke up and said, "My great-great grandfather once told me a story about a wonderful tree just like this one. It had the finest fruit but could only be reached by the ones who knew the name of the tree."

None of the animals knew the name of the tree and they all cried out, "But who can tell us the name of the tree?"

The wise, old tortoise said, "We must ask the king. The king will surely know the name of the tree."

"Let me go," said the swift gazelle. "I am the fastest of all the animals. I will run to the king and ask him the name of the tree." The gazelle ran off toward the jungle and before long found the king sitting beneath a tree beside a pond. The king saw the gazelle and asked, "Tell me why you are here, gazelle."

The gazelle said, "Mighty King, I have come a long way from where I left all the other animals who have gone in search of food. We are all very hungry and have found a tall tree with wonderful fruit. But we cannot eat the fruit until we know the name of the tree."

The lion said, "If I tell you the name of the tree, you must never forget because I will not tell you again. The name of the tree us Ungalli."

"Thank you, Mighty King, I will run as fast as I can to the others. So fast that I could not possibly forget the name of the tree, Ungalli."

The gazelle ran off across the great wide plain and so was nearing the tree and the other animals. Just before he reached them he stepped into a rabbits' hole in the ground. This made the gazelle fall while he was running faster than any animal could run. He tumbled and rolled, and rolled and tumbled until he came to a stop where the animals stood waiting.

The animals looked at the gazelle and asked, "Well, what's the name of the tree?"

The gazelle was dazed by having tripped in the rabbits' hole in the ground, and looked up at the animals and said, "I can't remember."

All of the animals moaned with hunger and sadness. "We must find someone else to go to ask the king the name of the tree," the all agreed.

"I will go this time," said the elephant. "My memory is the best of all the animals. I will not forget." All of the animals nodded their approval. And the elephant turned toward the jungle and started the long walk across the great wide plain.

When he came to the pond where the lion was resting, the elephant said, "Mighty King, I have come from . . ."

The lion said, "Wait, please don't tell me the gazelle forgot. You have come to learn the name of the tree, haven't you? The name of the tree is Ungalli. You must remember it because I will refuse to tell anyone else the name of the tree."

"Thank you," said the elephant, and start the long walk back to the other animals. "I will never forget because I never forget anything. In fact, I know the names of all the animals. And he began to name them out loud.

"I can even remember the names of all the birds in the jungle." And he began to name them, too, as he walked.

The elephant was just starting to name all of the stars in the sky when he stepped into the very rabbit hole that the gazelle step into. The elephant could not get his foot free. As all the animals waited for the elephant to get his foot free of the hole, one of them asked, "Elephant, what is the name of the tree?"

The elephant tugged and pulled and twisted until the foot came out of the hole. When he looked up at the other animals, he said, "I forgot." And all the animals moaned and cried with great hunger and disappointment.

The next to speak was a young tortoise. "I will go and bring back the name of the tree." The other animals said, "But, you are so small, you will tire easily, and you are so young, you will get lost and worst of all, you are so slow."

"Yes," said the turtle, "that is true. But, I know how to remember. I remembered the story about the tree, too."

The young tortoise began the long, slow walk all the way back to the jungle to ask the king the name of the tree. When the king saw the tortoise approaching, the fur on his back stood up and he growled loudly.

"If you have come to ask me the name of the tree, go away! I refuse to tell you. I have already told the gazelle and the elephant that the name of the tree is Ungalli. I will not tell you, too. So, go away!" The lion growled even louder than before.

The tortoise turned and walked away. As he walked, one foot after the other, he said over and over, "Ungalli, Ungalli, Ungalli . . ." He walked for the longest time on his way back to the tree and the other animals.

"Ungalli, Ungalli . . ." he said. As he approached the animals, he too, stepped into the rabbit hole and fell all the way to the bottom. A noise came up from the bottom of the hole, "Ungalli, Ungalli . . ." He was even saying it as he climbed all the way up and out of the deep rabbit hole. "Ungalli, Ungalli . . ."

The other animals were so tired and hungry that they did not even notice the young tortoise returning. As he walked up the animals all gathered under the tree, he looked up and said, "The name of the tree is Ungalli."

All the animals looked down at the tortoise and then up at the tree as the limbs slowly begin to bend down. The limbs bent so low the all of the animals could reach the wonderful fruit and the animals ate and ate. When they were finished, they lifted the young tortoise into the air and as the danced around the tree the all chanted, "Ungalli, Ungalli, the name of the tree is Ungalli," because they did not want to forget.

"ungalli"

Bev:*I don't know why it still surprises me but often when I hear a story some long lost memory from my childhood bubbles to the surface.*

Every time when I tell this story I think about the time . . .

I grew up in the Midwest in a large family. My Mom did not drive and, as I remember it, my Mom and Dad did their weekly shopping at the Piggley Wiggley. We also had a small local grocery just a few blocks from our house where we bought "stuff" during the week. Mom baked all her own bread and they grew and canned all the vegetables so we did not go the "neighborhood" store very often. I must have been about five when my Mom had a craving. She said, "Gosh, I would love a Snickers candy bar." I leapt to my feet and said, "I can go to the store!" After at least ten minutes of begging, she let me go. I had never crossed all those streets and I had never been to the store by myself. My heart was just pounding as I walked to the store. Imagine, I could do something really special for my Mom and go on an adventure at the same time. When I got to the store I had forgotten the name of the candy bar. Today, that doesn't seem so strange to me. I was so concerned about finding my way and pleasing my Mom no wonder I forgot the name. I ran home puffing and panting and I asked the name of the candy. At first she said, "Oh, never mind." I begged and pleaded and she let me go back. I ran as fast as I could and when I got there I had forgotten again! I think I went back and forth to the store three times. The third time the wonderful man who owned the store told me all the names of the candies. When he got to "Snickers" I knew. I have wondered since then why my Mom did not write the name of the candy bar down. Maybe she thought that would embarrass me. It was, as far as I can remember, the only time she ever sent me to the store for anything special. Mostly, it was for a necessity such as milk. I don't remember her giving me a bite of that candy bar. I do know I love Snickers.

I Am the Long One

Once upon a time, deep in the forest, there lived Rabbit. He was very clever and had built a most magnificent house. It had tall, straight walls, a heavy, strong door and a carefully worked, waterproof, thatched roof. Rabbit was very proud of his house. One day, he came home after working in the forest. As he was about to open his door, he heard a sound.

"Oh, dear," said Rabbit, "something is in my house!" He knocked on the door and this is what he heard, "I am the long one, I eat trees, and I walk on elephant's backs." Rabbit said, "Oh, dear, something really is in my house. Whatever shall I do?"

Just then, along came Turtle. "What's the matter, Rabbit?" said Turtle. Rabbit replied, "There's something in my house. Listen." He knocked on the door and they both heard, ""I am the long one, I eat trees, and I walk on elephant's backs."

"Hmmmm," said Turtle, "so there is. Would you like me to get it out of there?"

"You?" asked Rabbit. "You're so little and slow. What could you do? Go away, you're no help at all." So Turtle started to leave. He saw a nice log on the side of the road and decided to stay and watch what would happen next. He sat down, made himself comfortable and watched as along came Lion.

"What's the matter, Rabbit?" said Lion.

"Oh, there's something in my house. Listen," said Rabbit. And he knock on the door of his house and they both heard, "I am the long one, I eat trees, and I walk on elephant's backs."

"No problem," said Lion. "I'll just use my sharp claws and scrape down these walls. Then we'll see who's in there."

"Don't you dare," cried Rabbit. "I made those walls tall and straight and they are the best walls in the forest. Go away, you're no help at all." So, Lion shrugged and went on his way.

From out of the sky overhead came Eagle. "What's the matter, Rabbit," asked Eagle.

"Oh, the something in my house. Listen." And Rabbit knocked on the door of the house and they both heard, "I am the long one, I eat trees, and I walk on elephant's backs."

"No problem," said Eagle. "I'll just fly up above your house and pull off the roof. Then we'll see who's in your house."

"Don't you dare," cried Rabbit. "I made that roof carefully with thatch and it's the best roof in the forest. Go away, you're no help at all." So, Eagle shrugged and went on her way.

Next to come by was Hippopotamus. "What's the matter, Rabbit," asked Hippopotamus.

"Oh, the something in my house. Listen." And Rabbit knocked on the door of the house and they both heard, "I am the long one, I eat trees, and I walk on elephant's backs."

"No problem," said Hippopotamus, "I'll just lean against the door and push it in."

"Don't you dare," cried Rabbit. "I made that door heavy and strong and it's the best door in the forest. Go away, you're no help at all." So, Hippopotamus shrugged and went on his way.

All this time, Turtle had been watching. He called Rabbit over and said, "Are you sure you don't want me to try?" Rabbit said, "Well, nobody else had any good ideas, so I guess you might as well try."

So Turtle walked over to the house and knocked on the door and this is what they heard, "I am the long one, I eat trees, and I walk on elephant's backs."

"Oh, yeah," yelled Turtle, "well, I'm a Spitting Cobra and I'm going to crawl under the door and GET YOU!" There was silence from inside the house. Then very slowly, the door knob began to turn. Turtle and Rabbit watched as the door slowly creaked open and out came . . . Caterpillar. He was long, and he ate trees and he could even walk on the elephant's back. He looked at Turtle and Rabbit and said, "Hummpf. I don't know why you got so excited. I was just having a little fun." And he went off into the forest. Turtle and Rabbit watched him crawl away, looked at each other and shrugged and then went inside Rabbit's house and had dinner.

Kelly Anderson, a teacher at the Roseville Community Preschool, often tells this story and is great at modeling both flexibility and courage in it's telling: "In my version of this wonderful tale, the children decide what comes along the path next. And, it's not always an animal which can make it a bit challenging for me to create the rest of that part of the story. The kids love each thing I come up with to match their idea. For instance, one time a child said, 'An eyeball rolled down the path to Rabbit's house.' Well, that eyeball made a small hole in the thatched roof in order to see what was inside the house which Rabbit didn't like at all. As it turned out, that eyeball led to a whole story of body parts rather than animals."

The Tomorrow Monkeys

This story is about some monkeys that love to play. In fact, all monkeys love to play. Grown up monkeys, young monkeys, and baby monkeys -- they all love to play and will play from sunrise to sunset.

But when the sun goes down, the monkeys all climb up into the trees for the night. As they begin to fall asleep, the clouds roll in, and the rain starts to fall, and the wind begins to blow. And all the monkeys get very, very cold and they shiver all night long.

In the middle of the cold, wet night, the Papa monkey sits up and says, "Tomorrow, we will build a house."

And the Momma monkey says, "Yes, tomorrow, we will build a house."

And all the monkeys squeal, "Eeh - eeh - eeh - eeh - eeh - eeh."

In the morning, the sun comes up, the clouds roll away, and the monkeys all climb down from the trees to play under the bright blue sky. They play and play until one of the monkeys remembers, "Weren't we going to build a house today?"

And all the other monkeys say, "Later for that, later for that." And they all go back to their playing.

But when the sun goes down, the monkeys all climb up into the trees for the night. As they begin to fall asleep, the clouds roll in, and the rain starts to fall, and the wind begins to blow. And all the monkeys get very, very cold and they shiver all night long.

In the middle of the cold, wet night, the Papa monkey sits up and says, "Tomorrow, we will build a house."

And the Momma monkey says, "Yes, tomorrow, we will build a house."

And all the monkeys squeal, "Eeh - eeh - eeh - eeh - eeh - eeh."

In the morning, the sun comes up, the clouds roll away, and the monkeys all climb down from the trees to play under the bright blue sky. They play and play until one of the monkeys remembers, "Weren't we going to build a house today?"

And all the other monkeys say, "Later for that, later for that." And they all go back to their playing.

But when the sun goes down, the monkeys all climb up into the trees for the night. As they begin to fall asleep, the clouds roll in, and the rain starts to fall, and the wind begins to blow. And all the monkeys get very, very cold and they shiver all night long.

In the middle of the cold, wet night, the Papa monkey sits up and says, "Tomorrow, we will build a house."

And the Momma monkey says, "Yes, tomorrow, we will build a house."

And all the monkeys squeal, "Eeh - eeh - eeh - eeh - eeh - eeh."

In the morning, the sun comes up, the clouds roll away, and the monkeys all climb down from the trees to play under the bright blue sky. They play and play until one of the monkeys remembers, "Weren't we going to build a house today?"

Do you think they ever built that house?

The wonderful thing about this story is that is has no ending. Just go as long as you wish until finally asking, "Do you think they ever built that house?" The conversations that occur then usually show just how imaginative children can be. And, just like monkeys in this story, kids never want to quit their playing.

The line from the story, "Later for that" has been informally adopted by the parents and staff at our school as an acceptable response when things go a little crazy.

The Stone Cutter

Once upon a time there was a stone cutter. Everyday he would go to the mountains and cut stone with his hammer and his chisel.

"Chunk, chunk, chunk, chunk."

We he had cut a stone to the size he wanted, he would pick up the stone and put it in his cart. All day long he would cut stones.

"Chunk, chunk, chunk, chunk." And each time, when he was done, he would pick up the stone and put it in his cart. He cut and stacked stone day after day after day.
One day when the stone cutter was working, the sun began to beat down on him, and

he started to feel tired and sick. He said, "Sometimes, I wish I were a strong as the sun. The sun is very powerful."

It just so happened that nearby lived the Mountain Spirit. He has heard what the stone-cutter had said and he granted him his wish. The stone cutter became the sun!

"Oh, my," said the stone-cutter. "I am powerful and I can see everything there is to see. This is great."

Everything was great for the stone-cutter until one day when a cloud floated in front of the sun. He said, "Pardon me, but I cannot see when you are in front of me." But, the cloud did not move.

"Excuse me, Cloud!" But the cloud still did not move. The stone cutter Sun said, "I think I understand. The cloud is more powerful than the sun! If this is so, then I wish to be the Cloud." Just like that, the Sun became the Cloud.

Everything was great. He could rain on things to make them grow and he could make loud thunder when he was mad and he could even block the light of the sun if he wanted. Until one day when he wanted to float to another part of the sky. No matter how he tried, he could not move in the direction he wanted to go. It was because the Wind was blowing at him.

"Hey, Wind. Please stop blowing, I'm trying to go the other way." But the wind didn't stop. Again he asked but the wind kept blowing.

"Oh, I get it. The Wind is more powerful than the Cloud. If that is the case, then I wish to be the Wind." And just like that, he became the wind.

He loved being the Wind because he could go anywhere he liked and he could see everything he wanted to see. He was now sure he had to be the most powerful thing of all. That is until he ran into the Mountain.

He said, "Excuse me, Mountain, I am the Wind, please move out of my way so I can go where I please." But the mountain did not move at all. The stone-cutter thought about this, too.

"Oh, I think I get it. The mountain is the most powerful thing there is. I no longer wish to be the Wind, now I want to be the Mountain." And just like that, he became the Mountain.
Everything was great being the Mountain. When the sun shone, it warmed him up. And,

when it rained, it would cool him off. He finally knew he was the most powerful of all.

Until one day when he heard something and he felt something at his foot.

"Chunk, chunk, chunk, chunk."
"Chunk, chunk, chunk, chunk."

"Stop! That hurts. Who are you and what are you doing down there?" Mountain looked down at his foot and said, "Oh, I get it. The Stone-cutter is more powerful than the Mountain. I wish I were a stone cutter again. And just like that, he became a stone-cutter.

The next day, he went back to work happier than he had ever been.

"Chunk, chunk, chunk, chunk."
"Chunk, chunk, chunk, chunk."

A great message to children and aduts -- it's important to be who you are.

Grandma's Aprons - a quilt story

Many, many years ago there was a little boy named John. John grew up in the city and as most city boys of his time, his grandparents lived in the country. Every year John would go the country to live with his grandparents for a while.

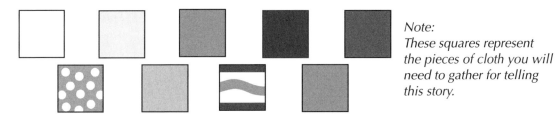

Note:
These squares represent the pieces of cloth you will need to gather for telling this story.

Life in the country was much different than John was used to. Every morning when John's grandparents got up the first thing they would do is to put on their work clothes. Grandpa would put on his overalls and Grandma would put on her apron. Grandma had many aprons; some were white, other were very colorful.

[white "apron"]

One day when John woke up it was cloudy and very rainy outside. He was mad that he had to stay inside to play.

"Why won't the sun to come out so I can go outside and play." John said.

Grandma smiled and said, "I'll make you a fun little playhouse where there will be many suns shining for you." She took her blue apron with circles of yellow and placed it over the backs of two chairs. John went inside the playhouse and happily played there all day long.

[blue w/ yellow circles]

The next day the sun came out and it was a pretty, blue-sky day. Grandma had on her white apron. Later that morning she asked John if he wanted to help her collect eggs from the hen-house. Grandma gathered her apron with one hand as to make a cloth basket. With the other hand she collect the eggs. John asked if he could do it, too. As he reached for the egg under a big, fat hen, the hen pecked at his hand. This scared John so that he threw the egg into the pile of eggs Grandma had collected in her apron. Many of the eggs broke and the yellow of the eggs soon spread throughout Grandma's clean white apron. Grandma tried to wash out the eggs but when you looked close you could still see that the apron was yellow in spots.

"That's okay. I've always wanted a yellow apron." And so she dyed it bright yellow.

 [yellow]

One day when Grandma and John were walking near the woods they discovered a patch of wild strawberries. John said, "I'll run back to the house a get a basket we can put the strawberries in." Grandma said, "That's not necessary. I have a basket right here in my apron." She held up the bottom corners and the apron formed a basket and they nearly filled it with the ripe red berries. When the got back to the farm house they emptied the strawberries out of the apron and noticed that the juice from the berries had stained the apron pink.

Grandmas said, "That's okay, I've always wanted a pink apron." And she dyed the apron bright pink.

[pink]

That weekend they decided to go on picnic. Grandma was wearing her Sunday apron --
- 110 -

the one trimmed in lace. When they got to the picnic site the realized they had forgot to bring a blanket to sit on. John noticed there were things crawling in the grass, like ants and bugs. Grandma said, "We can use this for a blanket." And she took off her apron and spread it on the ground. When they had finished eating they saw that the apron was green with grass stains.

"You know what, I've always wanted a green apron." And when they got home, she dyed the apron bright green.

[green]

The following day was the Fourth of July. Grandpa was going to march in the parade wearing his Army uniform. Grandma and John stood along side the road to watch the parade pass. John saw that many people had small flags to wave during the parade. He said, "I wish I had a flag to wave when Grandpa walks by."

Grandma took off her red, white and blue apron that she wore every Fourth of July and said to John, "You can wave this if you like." John smiled and his eyes got big as he took hold of one corner of the apron and Grandma held the other. When Grandpa passed by, they waved the flag together. Theirs was the biggest flag of all!

 [red, white & blue]

On Saturday was the day of the week when Grandpa always shined his shoes. John sat beside him to watch. When Grandpa was ready to buff the polish he asked John to bring him a polishing rag from the kitchen drawer. John ran in to the kitchen and opened a drawer and took a big white cloth to Grandpa. Neither Grandpa nor John noticed that the cloth was one of Grandma's bright white aprons.

When Grandma saw what they were doing she said, "Oh my, what are you two doing to my nice white apron?" Grandpa and John looked at each other and then at the apron that was now covered with brown streaks of shoe polish.

"Well, I've always wanted a nice brown apron," Grandma laughed. And she dyed the apron brown.

[brown]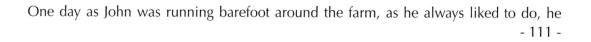

One day as John was running barefoot around the farm, as he always liked to do, he stepped on something sharp. "Ouch," he cried, "Grandma, I've think I cut my foot!" Grandma came running from the house. She could see that John's foot was bleeding and she quickly took off her apron and wrapped it around John's foot. She carried him into the kitchen and cleaned out the wound and put a bandage on the cut. When she looked at her apron with blood stains she said, "I don't think those stains will come out in the wash. But that's okay, besides I've always wished I had a red apron."

 [red]

Summer was nearly over and the day came for John to return to the city. John was sad to be leaving his Grandma and Grandpa but he couldn't wait to see his parents, too. Grandma held John as they road to town in their horse and buggy. She could tell he was getting cold so she took off her bright blue apron and wrapped it around John. Wrapped in Grandma's blue "going to town" apron, John fell fast asleep and dreamed of all the things he had done that summer on the farm.

[blue]

Years passed and John grew up, got married and had a family of his own. His Grandma and Grandpa had grown old and died. To help him remember his childhood days on the farm, John brought home with him all of Grandma's aprons. And he still has all of them to this day. Sometimes when he cooks, he puts on one of Grandma's aprons.

When John became a grandpa himself, he loved to tell his grandchildren stories of when he was little. He and his grandchildren would gather under the quilt he had made from pieces of Grandma's aprons. Each square reminded him of a story of his days on the farm and the times he was with his Grandma and Grandpa.

When I tell this story, I have added a part to the ending. Sometimes when people die their loved ones gather and share some of the things that their Grandparents owned that have a special meaning to them. Like the silverware or some of the furniture, etc., but all John wanted was Grandma's aprons. Sometimes the children will have stories to offer at this point when they have experienced a death in the family. Most people erroneously think this would make the children sad to recall such event. On the contrary, it has been my experience that they relish the opportunity to share such stories with their classmates.

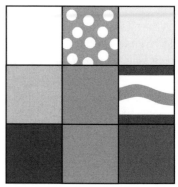

The Camping Story

This story evolved from our tradition of having a campout/slumber party that's held at the school during the spring. The families come with tents and sleeping bags, some sleep inside the school and some outside. We have a campfire for roasting marshmallows and singing and telling stories. Years ago I heard a similar story and added to it by adding details of those nights at the school campout. I just started with "Once there was a whole bunch of kids . . ."

Once there was a whole bunch of kids. They were all sleeping outside in the sleeping bags and tents. All except for Spencer, that is. As he lay there listening to the sounds of snoring and the wind, he all of a sudden smelled smoke! He sat up and sniffed the air. He was right, it was smoke!

"I think there's a forest fire!" He jumped up and quickly ran toward the smell of smoke.

> Down the road he went. (Slapping hands on thighs).
>
> Then over the bridge. (Beating chest with hands).
>
> Across the dry dirt. (Make sound by rubbing hands together).
>
> And, over the cobblestones. (Clicking sound with tongue).

Looking up at the top of the trees, Spencer could see fire. "It is a fire," he shouted. "I have to go back a get the other." So, he ran back toward camp.

> Over the cobblestones. (Clicking sound with tongue).
>
> Across the dry dirt. (Make sound by rubbing hands together).
>
> Back over the bridge. (Beating chest with hands).
>
> And, up the road he went. (Slapping hands on thighs).

When he got to camp he yelled, "Wake up, everybody. There's a forest fire! Wake up!" All of the kids jumped out of the sleeping bags and ran toward the smell of smoke.

> Down the road they went. (Slapping hands on thighs).
>
> Then over the bridge. (Beating chest with hands).
>
> Across the dry dirt. (Make sound by rubbing hands together).

And, over the cobblestones. (Clicking sound with tongue).

When they got there they all shouted, "You're right. There is a forest fire! What should we do?"

Spencer said, "We need water. Everybody back to camp and let's get out buckets. We'll fill them with water from the creek and then race back here and put this fire out."

"Yeah, let's go," they all shouted. So, back to camp they raced.

>   Over the cobblestones. (Clicking sound with tongue).
>   Across the dry dirt. (Make sound by rubbing hands together).
>   Back over the bridge. (Beating chest with hands).
>   And, up the road he went. (Slapping hands on thighs).

When the got back to camp, they grab their buckets and ran down to the creek. They quickly began filling the buckets with as much water as they could hold.

"That's plenty of water. Come on, let's go!" Spencer yelled. And as fast as they could, they high-tailed it back to the forest fire.

>   Down the road they went. (Slapping hands on thighs).
>   Then over the bridge. (Beating chest with hands).
>   Across the dry dirt. (Make sound by rubbing hands together).
>   And, over the cobblestones. (Clicking sound with tongue).

As they approached the fire Spencer hollered, "Everybody get ready with your buckets. On the count of three, we'll all throw the water on the fire together. Ready? ONE, TWO, THREE! THROW!"

Everyone threw, but nothing came out! There were holes in their buckets! "Now what are we going to do?" They a gasped.

"I've got an idea," Spencer yelled, "follow me!"

Spencer took off running back down the trail toward the creek with everyone right behind him.

> Over the cobblestones. (Clicking sound with tongue).
> Across the dry dirt. (Make sound by rubbing hands together).
> Back over the bridge. (Beating chest with hands).
> And, up the road he went. (Slapping hands on thighs).

As they got to the creek, Spencer said, "Okay, everyone start digging up the clay by the creekside and patch the holes in those buckets!" All the kids began digging furiously in the muddy mud and clay at the water's edge. They scooped up great globs of clay and slapped it on the holes in the buckets. Holding the up to the moonlight they could see that all the holes were now filled and they could once again hold water. So they filled the buckets and when everyone was ready, they sprinted back to the forest fire.

> Down the road they went. (Slapping hands on thighs).
> Then over the bridge. (Beating chest with hands).
> Across the dry dirt. (Make sound by rubbing hands together).
> And, over the cobblestones. (Clicking sound with tongue).

Spencer led them in putting out the fire by counting to three and they all gave a great mighty heave and the water washed over the entire forest -- putting out the fire completely. The only thing left to do was head back to camp -- only this time they went just a little bit slower.

> Over the cobblestones. (Clicking sound with tongue).
> Across the dry dirt. (Make sound by rubbing hands together).
> Back over the bridge. (Beating chest with hands).
> And, up the road he went. (Slapping hands on thighs).

The Story of the Little Bird and the Greedy Man

Once upon a time a little boy lived in the woods with his mother. They didn't have much money, just enough to put food on the table. The grew some fruits and vegetables in their garden. The little boy didn't have any toys either. He had to make them. He would make toys out of rocks, branches, or anything he could find on the ground around their house.

One day, the little boy went walking in the forest. He was looking for something to do. He looked and looked and looked, and then he saw a hurt bird laying on the ground. The little boy said, "I will take you home bird. My mama can make you better."

The little boy picked up the bird and carried it very gently home to his mother. "Mama, look what I found in the forest. A hurt bird," the little boy.

Mama looked at the bird and said, "Oh, my! This bird has a broken wing. I know just what this bird needs -- a splint." The boy's mama put a splint on the bird's wing and then wrapped the wing.

Everyday the little boy fed and gave water to the bird. Then the day come when the bird's wing was all better. It was time to set the bird free. The little boy thought, "Should I keep the bird for a pet or should I let him go so he can go back to his family and the other birds in the forest?"

Well, the boy decided to set the bird free. He walked outside with the bird cupped in his hands. He lifted them upward and the bird flew off. The bird circled around the sky above the boy. "Goodbye, bird. I know I will never see you again." As he waved, the bird flew off toward the forest.

The next morning, when the little boy got out of bed, there on the windowsill he saw the bird! The bird dropped a seed from out of its mouth and said, "This is for taking such good care of me," and then flew away. The little boy ran downstairs yelling, "Mama, Mama look what the bird gave me! A seed! I'm going to plant the seed in the garden!" He ran straight out to the garden and planted and watered the seed.

Everyday the boy tended the seed as it grew and grew. Soon it became a huge vine with melon growing on it. The boy couldn't wait to pick the melon because he and his mama would have a wonderful melon to eat. Finally, the day arrived when the melon was ripe enough to pick.

When the boy went to pick the melon, it was so ripe that it popped open and out something fell. The boy saw that they were coins! The melon was full of gold coins! The boy filled his pockets with the gold coins and ran to his mother.

"We're rich, we're rich! The melon was full of gold coins!" the boy yelled. We'll never have to worry about money ever again!"

Soon, the word of the boy's good fortune spread throughout the town. Everyone was talking about the little boy and the gold coins. Everyone, including the very greedy man who lived in that same town. He couldn't believe someone could be richer than he. The greedy man asked everyone he met, "How did that little boy get so rich?"

The townspeople told the greedy man the story of how the boy found the hurt bird and cared for it and that the bird had brought the boy a seed that grew a huge vine. And the boy, having planted the seed, grew a melon that was full of gold. The greedy man couldn't believe such a story so he decided to go to the boy's house and find out for himself.

The greedy man walked across that woods and when he got to the little boy's house he knocked on the door. The boy opened the door and the greedy man said, "Tell me, little boy, how did you get so rich?"

The boy told the greedy man the whole story of how he was walking in the woods and how he found the hurt bird. He told him how he gently took the bird home and his mama had fixed its wing and how he had fed and gave water to the bird everyday. When the bird was well, he set it free. The next day, the bird returned and brought him the seed that the vine and melon that was filled with gold coins.

The greedy man thought, "I could find a hurt bird and take care of it." So, off he went in to the forest to find a hurt bird. He looked and he looked but he couldn't find one anywhere. He thought, "I've got an idea." And he picked up a rock and threw it at a bird flying overhead. The rock hit the bird and the bird dropped to the ground!

The greedy man ran to the bird and said, "Oh, you poor thing, you're hurt. I'll take you home and make you all better."

The greedy man took care of the bird. He fed and gave water to the bird everyday. When the day came to set the bird free, the greedy man said, "Goodbye, bird. "I'll miss you."

The next morning, the bird was sitting on the windowsill of the greedy man's house. He dropped a seed out of his mouth and said, "This is for what you did to me," and he quickly flew away.

The greedy man rubbed his hands together and laughed, "I'll plant this seed and then I'll be richer. I'll even have more money than that little boy and his mama." He planted the seed and watered it everyday. In no time at all, a vine grew and on it was a huge melon. The vine and the melon grew and grew. And, finally, the day came when the melon was ripe enough to pick. When the greedy man reached to pick up the melon, it too was so ripe that it split open and out popped . . . WORMS!

From Sally Hupp, a teacher at the Roseville Community Preschool: "This is one of my favorite stories to tell the children. Its an age-old story of right and wrong, good and bad and the way I tell it, the story has a pretty tasty ending. But first, let me tell you something about how I involve the children. At the very start of the story, when I'm describing the little boy, his mama and their garden, often the children will spontaneously tell me what kind of vegetables they might have grown or they might tell me they don't like vegetables. When you ask a question like, "What do you think they grew?" -- or any question for that matter, practice remembering where you were and how to pick up the story once the kids have had a chance to speak their mind.

The caring of the bird and the splinting of its wing ususally result in some conversation, too. Sometimes I ask them if they know what a splint is or they might share with me a story of when they got hurt or bandaged. When the greedy man hurts the bird, I use a most disgusted tone when I say, "Oh, brother! He hurt the bird and now he's going to take him home!"

For the ending when the ripe melon pops open, I have ready to go a big bag of gummy worms to hand out to the children while I say, "Worms, worms! The melon was full of worms!"

Bev Bos --

Has taught preschool children for over 35 years at the Roseville Community Preschool. She has authored four books for teachers and parents, produced two DVDs, and nine CDs of music for young children with Tom Hunter and her son-in-law, Michael Leeman.

Her passion for teaching a creativity has made her a much sought after speaker for parent's groups, schools, and education conferences for many years.

Her latest book, ***Tumbling Over the Edge - a rant for children's play,*** co-authored by Jenny Chapman, focuses on the importance of play in childhood.

Bev lives in Roseville Ca., with her husband Bob and has five children, fourteen grandchildren and two great-grandchildren.

Michael Leeman --

Musician and Illustrator. Besides his collaboration with Bev Bos on this book of chants and stories, Michael has also illustrated ***Morningtown Ride***, a children's picture book version of the popular Malvina Reynold's lullaby. His illustrations have appeared in other books and publications as well including ***Tumbling Over the Edge - a rant for children's play***, authored by Bev Bos and Jenny Chapman.

Michael also works as Music Teacher at the Roseville Community School for children K--6th. He lives in Roseville Ca., with his wife Carrie and their daughters, Meghan and Jillian.

Bev Bos and Michael Leeman have worked together for over twenty years throughout the United States and Canada presenting seminars and workshops for parents and early childhood educators. They also perform music for community concerts and schools assemblies and have worked together on many books and articles published through Turn the Page Press, Inc., which Bev founded in 1977.

For information on how you can contact Bev or Michael, or for information regarding workshops, concerts, books, music and toys for young children, please call Turn the Page Press, Inc. at 1-800-959-5549 or visit their website at www.turnthepage.com.